Adventures of Ojemba

The Chronicle of Igbo People

Chukwuma J. Obiagwu

Hamilton Books
A member of
The Rowman & Littlefield Publishing Group
Lanham • Boulder • New York • Toronto • Plymouth, UK

Adventures of Ojemba: Chronicle of Igbo People is written in memory of Arufo alias Ojemba whose full name was Nze Iroegbuba Alphonsus Obiagwu. He departed this earth on September 1, 1997. He deserved the name Ojemba for he was the adventurer and the master storyteller. Being the Ojemba's child I was used to those stories and taught very little about them. However, when my wife, Loretta visited Nigeria he asked questions about the people she saw. Arufo opened up as usual. She took note and found his stories very interesting and demanded that we do something about it. She wanted her friends and colleagues to be able to experience such rich information she was privileged to have. This book is dedicated to both individuals.

Contents

Foreword

There are traditional storytellers in every African tribe. Such storytellers are called "Groits". The office of Groit, like a kingdom, is handed down to descendants, who trace their lineage from man through God to the smallest grain of sand. The Groit tells the history of a tribe such as their anxieties, frustrations, hopes, doubts and even the desires of their people. The Groit tells the story or the oral history of his people. But sometimes the narrator and the story become synthesized or metamorphosed. This means that sometimes it is difficult to try to separate the narrator, the Groit, from the story. This sentiment may remind us of what W. B. Yeats implied when he said that *"it is sometimes difficult to separate the dance from the dancer"*

This foreword hints at the theme and narrative of Ojemba: The Adventurer. Dr. Chukwuma Obiagwu narrated the story told by *Arufo,* the village Groit. However, Dr. Obiagwu became the narrator's narrator, a *mimesis* of the original Groit, Arufo. This story eventually became Dr. Chukwuma Obiagwus' story. The story of the genealogy of the family line with all the frustrations, anxieties, hopes, doubts and desires. It is also the story of *Igbo people* described as wonderers, scattered around the world. In a way, one Igbo man's story is the communal and universal story of the entire tribe of people with similar ways of life.

Emmanuel Egar, PhD
Professor of English & formally the
Head of English Department, University
of Arkansas at Pine Bluff.

Preface

OJEMBA: THE ADVENTURER

Arufo, the Ojemba told stories for every situation, some of which were left as legacy to his own children. He told how a beautiful queen of Egypt was turned into a python when she challenged her personal spirit and that the royal python which Igbo people revered until recently was that queen called *Ikutu. Arufos* stories are mostly of kings and queens of kingdoms and empires his people never heard of even when names he named sounded familiar. He mentioned places like *Egypt, Ethiopia, Saba or Asaba, Nubia or Unubi-Igbo, Igbo-Ukwu, Aguleri, Ohambi, Utonkon, Igede, Akputu, Mumchi, Uguta, Ijebu Igbo etc.* As a child I did not believe these places are in this present world but as an adult I seem to have visited most of the places mentioned in his stories. Some however do not exist any longer. In all those stories, it was either his father told him or he was there and the people told him.

So *Arufo,* the holder of the highest *Ozo* title in his community, was mocked occasionally with the name *Ojemba.* When he told stories of Saba, Ethiopia and Nubia from where his ancestors originated and ruled the world at various periods in ancient times in history, I was amused because they were entertaining but more than that they were educative. Their educational values to me were as folk tales for which Igbo traditions were famous. When I became older, read more of the ancient history, I realized that what Ojemba told was really histories of different people at different times. There was really Ethiopia as well as an empire called Saba, there was Nubia, which conquered the ancient world at the same time a Roman Emperor named Nero, the stepson of Claudius, was in power. Of course there is Egypt, although presently overtaken by the Arabs and Greeks, was a Black African Nation.

Of all his stories, the most significant was that of the *ADWA,* the daughter of Akeze and great grandchild of Kedema the last child of Ishmael who became the first ruler of Independent Saba (Hebrew 'Sheba'). The story of this great queen as told by Ojemba seemed unlikely to be a reality but it was. *Ojemba* told the story of burial tomb of the queen, which was brought to the present day Asaba (West of River Niger Delta of Nigeria), after the fall of the Nubian Empire. He said that the tomb became a sanctuary of worship for some Igbo people especially the *IKAI-Igbos.* However, during the world economic recession that occurred around 1930s to 1940s, British colonialists established a lumber company between Sapele and Ijebu area of the present day Western Nigeria, as the subsidiary of 'United African Company (UAC)'. Many Igbo people including *Ojemba* went for the *"Igedu Job"* as it was called. Also went in search of jobs were the high priests of the tomb sanctuary. As they went, they established another sanctuary where they laid the remains of the queen in the eastern part of Ijebu Ode. This part of the town was later named Ijebu Igbo because of the presence of large population of Igbo lumber workers in the place.

When *Ojemba* was asked if the sanctuary could still be found, he mentioned that the white mans religion helped to destroy the sanctuary housing the tomb of the great queen. And that in fact, the British stole all the rich artifacts while the keepers of the sanctuary were forced to convert to European Christianity. These stories could have been a folk tale but for one event in early 1999. As I was flipping through the Internet, I saw an article, which stated that archeologist located the tomb of the great queen of Sheba exactly where Ojemba described it. By this time Arufo had been long dead which means that he did not base his story on such finds but from his personal observations during the 1930s.

In general, *Chronicle of Igbo People* is divided into four main sections with a total of nine chapters. Each section is opened with original tales of Ojemba about his people. Each chapter is subdivided into sections and subsections where necessary. Section one gave, not in chronological order, the origin of Igbo people. This single Chapter section was partially based on the *"Tales of Ojemba"* which motivated this project. It was tales of kingdoms, empires, kings and emperors suspected to be Igbo ancestors in the ancient times.

Section two containing chapters 2 through 4 are detailing Igbo peoples' culture and traditions that makes them what they are. The section shows that Igbo People were very religious even before the coming of Europeans. They believed in the supremacy of one God which they described as a creator or indescribable mighty spirit. The section also gave some insight of family roles and relationships including the use of proverbs and idioms in general communication. Economically, Igbo People are force to be reckoned with.

Section three consisting of Chapters 5 and 6 is describing what the people do to make a living especially in their homeland. They are first and foremost agrarian people, then they traded on food products, and subsequently they manufactured goods and rendered important services to the entire Nigerian nation. They were natural partners to the Europeans who helped them to expand their markets.

Section four containing chapters 7, 8 and 9 is portraying Igbo people in the light of what the compilers of the "Universal Illustrated Encyclopedia believed about them." They had stated, "With the coming of the Europeans, Igbo people quickly adapted and became a powerful political and economic force in Africa." That characteristic is also playing a significant role in their adaptation to new environments in Asia, Europe and North America. The same section also listed the people's partnership with the colonialists and subsequently, their demand for Independent, not for Igbo Nation but for amalgamations of different tribes in the River Niger basins. In other words, they created Nigeria with the active collaboration of British Royal Niger Company when other tribes were reluctant to enter into such amorphous union. When they ended up as the economic backbone of the larger nation, it became necessary for them to rethink their membership of the union. They tried to reclaim their independence from Nigeria in the 1960s by creating the Independent State of Biafra. They are currently up in arms with Nigeria where MASSOB is demanding for a peaceful separation from Nigeria. It is still a Herculean task but they believe that it can be achieved.

Igbo leaders and brief description of their roles in development or destruction of Igbo land were chronicled. Important towns, some which was described in the text were also listed. Finally, as this book was initially published in the internet in the year 2000, several individuals critiqued the essay and urged for its production as a book. This attempt therefore is to fulfill that request made by discussants at Biafra-Nigerian Message Board, described as the voice of new generation.

Chukwuma J. Obiagwu, PhD
Director of Technology, Hall High School,
Little Rock School District &
The General Secretary
Ndigbo in Arkansas, (a non-profit organization for
the advancement of Igbo Culture and Heritage in Arkansas).

Section 1

THE ORIGIN OF IGBO PEOPLE

OJEMBA STORY

Igbo people came into existence through a man called Ukeneme the son of Nwachukwu. Nwachukwu, Ukeneme's father, was called God's son because his earthly father abandoned him few years after he was born. An angel of the Lord was sent from heaven to adopt him on behalf of God. He was however to inhabit the forest, fight nature and wilderness in order to become a strong man. He eventually conquered the forest and his descendants became forest people where kings and queens emerged to rule the ancient world at various times. Ukeneme was actually the last son of Nwachukwu. He founded the settlement of Asaba-Igbo near Ethiopia and married an Ethiopian princess. His great grand daughter called Ada became the queen of Asaba. Her son became the Menelik 1, an emperor of unified Ethiopia while her other generations ruled at Aksum, Unubi-Igbo, Cush, and even Egypt. The Emperors or kings of Unubi-Igbo created important cities such as Maarib, Aksum, Adwa, Meroe, Ahiaragu, Enugu etc., on their way to their promised land. There may have been about 44 Ukeneme dynasties that ruled the world of Igbo people.

Arufo

Chapter One

The Origin of Igbo People

INTRODUCTION

In this Chapter, Ojemba would try to answer an expected question; *who is the Igbos?* The book will try to provide the answer by developing a theory based on Ojemba's Tales. Igbo people are therefore the generation of people that developed Aksum, Cush, Nubia, Sheba etc., originating from the horn of Africa (North East of the Sub Continent). They had moved to the Central and then to West Africa because these various kingdoms and empires declined and because they remained strangers among indigenous people whom they had ruled. They encountered several revolts because they were strangers and some of such revolts often became catastrophic, necessitating relocation. They were therefore able to establishment several communities in many regions. This book also tried to imply that some of such movements were really ordained in order that they finally find the Promised Land, i.e. where they are today.

WHY OJEMBA STORY COULD NOT BE IGNORED

Igbo people are black and the original stock of humans created in the world before the great flood. With reference to a Newsweek[1] article sometime in 1988, there is a possibility that the first human on the planet before and after Noah's Ark or indeed those who survived the great flood were a single original black group. The Ark must have been built in Africa where it was possible to have obtained various breed of livestock and pair of every crop to regenerate the world after the flood. In the articles, pictures of Black Adam and

3

Eve were shown on the front cover which captures the thesis of the article as reflected in the findings of DNA researchers. This discovery may in fact be a confirmation that the original woman and man as the first fruits of humanity's creation were indeed black.

The scientists presented their "Eve" as most likely a *"dark-haired, black skinned woman."* They traced her through International assortments of genes and followed a trail of DNA that led them to a single woman from whom they believed all humans are descended. Their evidence indicated that Eve lived in "Sub-Saharan Africa." The researcher went on to say that the DNA of the babies tested appeared to form a family tree, which was rooted in Africa. One category of this DNA data was found only in some babies of recent African descent. A second category was found in everyone else and the other African people. So these researchers concluded that the DNA tree began in African, from which a group of Africans emigrated thus splitting off to form a second branch of DNA, which they carried into the rest of the world. Regardless of which category, all the babies' DNA was traceable back, ultimately to one woman.

If Adam was from Africa, then all people are "African" in one sense, for all people are derived from, according to the scriptures, one common ancestor-Adam; *"God's Adam who physically must have been gloriously colorful, for he was created in the image of God from the dust of the ground."* It is a noted fact that wherever ancient civilizations have emerged on the face of the earth, they were black. Whether in Nubia, Cush, Summer, Asia Minor, North America or South America, the center of culture of the ancient world was "Hermitic in Origin." Blacks are the progenitors of humanity and the creative originators of culture and civilization. The existence of whiteness and the development of "white" people occurred later in the history of humanity. In other words, the Biblical-evidence, archaeological evidence and DNA-wise evidence points in the direction that Blackness is humanity's norm while whiteness is the exception rather than the rule. White skin is therefore the deviation from the original humanity. At death all colors are reverted to blackness and eventually to dust.

IGBO'S HEBREW CONNECTION

In the land of Canaan of the ancient Middle East, Hagar, a black woman from Africa was married to Abraham, a Jewish nomad. While starvation and famine descended on the Abraham's country, he sought and obtained help from benevolent Africans in Egypt. Not only that he was fed, the great Pharaoh bequeathed him with gifts including male and female servants (Gen.

12:16). Hagar, the daughter of blacksmith called Naradush was one of the female servants who accompanied Abraham and Sarah to the land of Canaan. She became the handmaid of Sarah and managed Abraham's family with great efficiency. She never was a slave, for Abraham neither bought her nor captured her in any warfare according the Bible. Because Sarah was barren for most of her life, she gave her handmaid to Abraham to marry as second wife. The purpose was for him to have children who would bear his name after him. Ironically however, Sarah was enraged when Hagar became pregnant for Abraham and eventually had a son, named Ishmael. Abraham was forced by Sarah to abandon this child and his mother.

God however, intervened and gave a promise of a son also to Sarah probably to calm her down. God then instructed Abraham to accept and care for Hagar and her son. The seed of discord had been sown and Ishmael had to be abandoned in favor of Isaac in the house of Abraham but not in the sight of God. Ishmael grew in the wilderness and married in the house of Gush, descendant of Naradush, his mother's lineage. The Bible recorded that he married two other women (1Chr. 1:29–31). Ishmael settled at Havilar-Shur across the Mediterranean at the eastern part of Egypt as you go towards Assyria (Gen. 25:18). When he died at the ripe age of one hundred and thirty seven years, his twelve sons had multiplied exceedingly as promised by God (Gen. 21:13). Each son established different settlement that grew into tribes. Holy Bible named the twelve tribes of Ishmael as Nebojoth, Keder, Adbeel, Mispan, Mishma, Dumah, Massa, Hadad, Tema, Teture, Naphish and Kedema in the order of their birth (1Chr. 1: 29–31). As the Havilar-Shur was a territory of Egypt, the descendants of Ishmael were regarded as strangers in the land. Although they were made to live by the rule of law established for Egyptians, they were allowed a great deal of autonomy, which enabled them to establish their own systems of preserving their Jewish traditions.

UKENEME (HEBREW, KEDEMA) IN SABA PROVINCE

Kedema was the youngest child of Ishmael. When his father died, he was only 12 years old. On the other hand his oldest brother, Nebojoth, was 86 years old. After the death of Ishmael, all his wealth was divided among the adult children excluding Kedema. He was therefore unable to inherit any of his father's wealth. To survive, he had to serve his brother, Hadad, the first child of his own mother, for seven years. When he was barely 20 years he set out to be on his own. Hadad had taught him to be a trader as well as crop farmer. He traded on goods and commodities brought by sea merchants. He traveled to distant lands for commercial purposes. Some of his trading sprees took him to Saba (now republic of Yemen), a province of Ethiopia, and south of their original settlement (Havilar-Shur). Saba, Hebrew Sheba, an ancient kingdom directly East of Ethiopia across the Red sea and Gulf of Anden mentioned in the Bible, most notably in the story about the meeting between King Solomon and the Queen (See 1 King 10: 1–13).

Kedema found the Saba land very fertile that he decided to start a settlement with his servants and nephews that were with him. While in Saba, he continued to trade on goods and commodities produced in Egypt and other countries. Fifteen years after his arrival in the land of Saba, he married the daughter of an Emperor of Ethiopia. In about 10 century BC, Saba, an Ethiopian province grew into a remarkable trading center and it became known all over the ancient world. With the marriage to the princess of Ethiopia, Kedema's Saba was given relative autonomy.

THE RISE OF ADWA (ADA): THE QUEEN OF SABA

Kedema's great grand daughter *"Adwa"* later became the queen of Saba. Under her leadership, Saba grew in leaps and bounds. With the wealth and influence of Adwa and her descendants, Saba became one of the most powerful states in Southern Arabia until 115 BC, when Himyarites gained ascendancy. During the rule of Adwa descendants however, the chief city occupied the present day Maarib, east of Sana'a, the capital of Yemen. At the height of its development, in the 8th century, the kingdom of Saba maintained colonies along trade routes leading to Palestine. Maarib became one of the wealthiest cities of the ancient world.

EMERGENCE OF EMPEROR EZANA

After Adwa as the queen of autonomous Saba, her son Menelik 1 united Saba with Ethiopia and became the emperor of larger Ethiopia. Years later, Saba was lost and a new emperor called Ezana moved his capital to Aksum. Ezana's descendants ruled Ethiopia until 50 AD. During those periods, Ethiopia showed evidence of influence from Southern Arabia in its spiritual beliefs, its language and it's writing until Ezana V was converted to Coptic Christian. He made the religion the state religion. During the 4th century, Greek influences began to predominate. Ethiopia's receptiveness to outside influences was largely a result of the Kings continued contact with his cousins in the Lower Egypt.

The country's shoreline on the Red sea and the Gulf of Anden made it a natural port for ships sailing from Egypt to trade with India and the Far East. The Ethiopian port of Adulis on the Red sea was a vital link in trade between Africa, the Mediterranean nations and Asia. From the interior, Caravans brought iron, animals, gold, horns, slaves and tortoise shells. These they traded for weapons, cloth, wine and other local products. Adulis was cosmopolitan city with residents from Egypt, Persia and India. Greek was frequently spoken there. King Ezana V became the most powerful king in East Africa.

NUBIA: GATEWAY TO CONTINENTAL AFRICA

Historical accounts indicated that the people from Saba were responsible to the spread of Neolithic civilization, which their cousins helped to establish in Egypt. They thus became the main link between the Europeans and Africans in the 4th century. Aksum was strong as a nation well into the 7th century, when the kings forged alliances with several Byzantine emperors. Muslim however, gained control of most of the surrounding territory and forced Aksum off the Arabian Peninsula. Aksum quickly declined in importance, although it stubbornly maintained its traditions through the centuries. The spread of iron culture southwards into the African continent was consistent with the movement of people from Saba and Aksum. In the hinterland, the region of modern day Sudan, these people set up a black nation called Nubia (Negro Africans). Nubian empire extended from the Mediterranean South to the borders of Ethiopia and possibly into modern day Uganda. For a brief period, Nubia was one of the most powerful empires in the world. Large slagheaps from ancient times indicate that the Nubians used smelting irons. They appear to have been active traders, exporting metal goods including gold, Ivory and iron deep into Africa and to places as remote as Greece, Rome and Algeria. During the 1st century AD, after the Romans conquered Egypt, Nubia sent ambassadors to Rome. The emperor, Nero, returned the favor by sending an ambassador to Meroe, Nubian's capital. It is possible that Nubia, through its trade, served as a kind of clearinghouse for passing on ideas from Mediterranean civilization to the more remote areas in Africa.

Other artifacts left by Nubians are impressive. They built burial mounds in the fashion of the Egyptian pyramids. Near the capital city of Meroe, they may have been more that 60 of such royal mound (tombs). They are as many as 200 Mereotic sites in Sudan today, but only a few had been studied. Those studied provided hint of life of larger civilization. The discovery of Nubian spindle whorls suggests that the people wove cotton garments. Among the most remarkable artifacts from Nubia are superb earthenware designs. The discovery of fine pottery even in the smaller villages suggests that the empire enjoyed high degree of prosperity as well as artistry. Mereotic wheel turned pottery is considered some of the finest from the ancient world.

NUBIAN EXPANSION

Internal wrangling among others was responsible for the decline of Nubia. They were initially overshadowed and sometimes ruled by Pharaohs of Egypt when the Adwa ruling house was not able to bring their acts together. However, in 725 BC, Piankhy, descendant of Adwa gained power with the decline of the Pharaohs as the emperor of Nubia. He conquered Egypt, thus establishing the 25th ruling dynasty in Egypt. Apart from power struggle among the descendants of Kedema, Nubia was defeated in war by the Assurbanipal. Because of that defeat, the emperor shifted his capital southward specifically falling back to Napata at the fourth cataract (or waterfalls) of the Nile, then to Meroe beyond the fifth cataract. The emperor defeated the Cushites at Meroe and established the city as his second capital.

They came to Meroe with their entrepreneur skills and made a once sleeping city, a thriving commercial center of the world. The movement of Kedema tribe was traced from Aksum to Meroe at about 750 BC, to Napata below the 4th cataract in the earlier 6th century. As Meroe became the center of iron smelting, it maintained a leading role in the iron market. In roughly AD 350, the Adwa dynasty was overthrown by the nomads and by rival merchants. The civilization however, may have been weakened by over population and subsequent demand upon the fragile vegetation of the region.

JOURNEY TO CENTRAL AND WEST AFRICA

As soon as the empire of Nubia declined, the inhabitants started moving to the Central and West African sub regions in search for markets and fertile lands and to associate with emerging empires of Ghana, Songhay and Mali. The journey was through Darfur down to the Congo basin and across the Cameroon Mountains. The people were alternatively called Kwa-eboa people as they were said to speak Kwa languages.

They were traders and ironworkers, making them the pioneers of modern technologies across Africa. They helped to build cities as trading posts mainly to serve their commercial interests. They were able to settle in many parts of Africa, some of, which became extinct while most have been lost to other people of different races. The indication was that the Kwa language is the largest among the various subfamilies of Niger-Congo languages spoken in the Central and West Africa. In Nigeria alone, the Kwa subfamily of languages formed the various ethnic groups such as Tiv, Idoma, Doma, Nupe, Igala, and Efik while the largest is Ibo. The customs and traditions of these tribes overlapped. In general, they are basically crop farmers, producing root crops and other commodities. They are also commercially oriented and highly mobile.

Varieties of domesticated crops as well as breeds of animals typically found in Egypt and the Asian Continent were introduced to the sub region by these immigrants. In Congo Basin of Central Africa there were no indications that crop agriculture was practiced before the arrival of Saba people. In West African, so many hundreds of years after their arrival, all the domesticated animals with exception of guinea fowl, seem to have been borrowed from the North East Africa sub region. They were also responsible for the introduction of iron technology with abundant number of metallurgical workers known as blacksmiths among them. Archeological artifacts found in various West African locations, especially of metal hoe, were said to be the sign of the presence of the Kedema tribe or Saba people.

The large stock of Kwa language groups in Africa continent indicated that the Nubians arrived in the location at different period and often relocated to new areas once in a settlement. This helped them to acquire the capacity to adapt to new environment. By their wide spread especially in the modern day Nigeria, they have made valuable contribution to the creation of modern Africa. Their ability to move and resettle in many lands was foretold Biblically. For God has said to Abraham after the birth of Ishmael, "Know certainly that your descendants shall be strangers in land that are not theirs for 400 years" (Gen. 15:13). They helped to create nations after nations and because they were strangers, they were never absorbed in the process. Wherever they have settled, their cultural heritage helped set them apart from their host community. They have been able to govern themselves even without established kingdoms.

IGBO AND NUBIAN (SABA) CULTURE COMPARED

The Saba people otherwise the Nubians, even in their most recent settlements in Central and West Africa, worshiped only the creator. Unlike the ancient Greek and Romans, their leaders never assumed the role of gods and therefore the people never worshiped them. They believed in the existence of the Supreme God who delivered their forefather Ishmael from the wilderness of the Mediterranean deserts. They also believed in supernaturalism, in ancestral protections, in mystic potency of certain persons and in spirits of several kinds, who they suppose were subordinates to God. Some of the spirits are assumed to be both physical and spiritual messengers of God. The Nubian immigrants in West Africa had great respect for age and experiences and organized their leadership in that direction. They lived in numerous autonomous families once sacked from Nubia, their last empire or kingdom. These autonomous families often grew into villages and towns with time. They maintained special links with their ancestors and ancestral heritage. They had no standing army while they became the husbandry of most civilization in Africa. They practiced advance economy of food production and in fact some of their philosophers became scholars in the Ancient University of Timbuktu. They engaged in considerable amount of trade with distant markets. They used masks to celebrate their festivities. They were artistic and there were art works for every expression, perhaps borrowed from Egypt. These art works are indispensable elements of their religion, which are also used as spiritual symbols concerned with agriculture, ancestors, divination and secret societies. Igbo people of West Africa are completely associated with the above culture. They are therefore, the largest part of the Kwa-speaking people who left Nubia after its decline to establish new settlements in Central and West Africa. The commercial efforts of Igbo people helped to build cities such as Jos, Yaunde, Accra, Cotonou, Kaduna, Kano and Maiduguri.

ARRIVING AT THE PROMISED LAND

What ever was the real reason for the fall of Nubia became a catalyst for the people to relocate to what they believe was their Promised Land in West Africa. Igbo people reside in the modern day Eastern Nigeria as well as the Niger Delta regions. The area had been a Promised Land for the Kedema descendants because it was mainly a tropical forest and according to God's injunction, they have to be forest people. It is the eastern part of the Gulf of Guinea, which is literally flowing with petroleum oil and natural gas with very rich agricultural lands. It is bordered in the East by the Central African Republic, including Cameroon, and in the South by small Islands of Bioko (formerly Fernando Po). It is also bordered in the West by the Ancient Benin Kingdom, (now Edo State of Nigeria). Its principal ports were Port Harcourt, Calabar, Douala and Cameroon. Douala and Cameroon were however removed from Igbo land by the government of Alhaji Tafawa Balewa in 1962. The principal cities are Enugu, Port Harcourt, Onitsha, Aba, Owerri, Awka,

Abakaliki, Umuahia, Asaba, Orlu, and Okigwe, each of which was provincial headquarters before the creation of 37 states in Nigeria.

Before arriving to the now homeland, these Saba people were first settled in Congo Basin from where they moved to the Cameroon mountains. They were said to have located the homeland by about AD 200. When they arrived, the place was unoccupied by any race and they were convinced that they have reached the Promised Land. The conviction was partly justified by the existence of large body of water (Atlantic Ocean) at the extreme south. By the sight of the water, they assumed that they were destined to stop so far and claim the land especially as they were no other people disputing their claim at the time. Archeology provided evidence that the people were the same pioneering group of the ancient Saba immigrants who spread the knowledge and the use of iron implements in various African locations. They also played vital roles, as middlemen with kings and emperors, providing needed European and Arabian goods to the local population.

Archeological finds in the Jos Plateau of the present day Nigeria indicates that Nubia people lived in the area from 500 BC. Iron tools and cast bronze burial artifacts from Nubia culture provided the earliest evidence of the Iron Age in West Africa. During the 19th century, Fulani chief and Islamic leader named Usman Dan Fodio (Shehu) carried out series of wars he called Jihad in the region. The Nubian immigrants, otherwise the descendants of Ishmael retreated to the Ekoi/Ogoja axis to avoid incursion by Fulani horsemen. From this area they traded with Hausa kingdoms. The more southward movement was completed then in order to avoid being forced to Islamic faith.

SPREAD OF IGBO PEOPLE IN AFRICA AND WORLD

Although they were no records to show that they created other empires after the fall of Nubia, they however played vital roles in nearby empires as middlemen in distribute trade. They were rarely involved in local politics and although they did not take direct orders from these host empires or kingdoms, they submitted to the rule of laws that did not contradict their traditions and culture. As pioneers in many fields of commerce, their influences were felt throughout Africa. In the 18th century, when the British formed "The Royal Niger Company," these people became natural partners in business. Because they did not have kings, they felt unconcern when the British colonized the provinces around the Niger River Basins as the 'Southern Protectorate'. These were also important to the local population whom they provided the services.

They were not shielded from aggressions of the local population. However, they were able to resist such aggressions through voluntary military services, as they kept no standing army. They raised volunteers when necessary. However, they tried as much as they could to keep out of many wars by moving on or by negotiations. Their ability to negotiate notwithstanding, there was several instances where external aggression had to be put down. Sometimes they succeeded and sometimes they failed. In many occasions they avoided confrontation by moving on to new, secure or more friendly environments until certain factors limited those securities. There was no standing army because there was no taxation and sources of common revenue to care for a disciplined army. The result was the incessant attack on their villages. Most of the time, villages may be sacked before volunteers could be ready to counter the attacks.

NOTE

1. Reference to the January 11, 1988 *Newsweek* article entitled *"The Search for Adam & Eve."*

Section II

CULTURE OF IGBO PEOPLE

OJEMBA STORY

There are many things that constitute abomination in Igbo Land. People are forbidden from committing abomination such as killing not only of a fellow human being but some sacred animals in designated places. Because they have been through a lot and traveled so far to their present settlement, they became their own brother's keepers. They were no pagans as far as people believe in one God is concerned even before the coming of Irish Catholicism and other European Christianity. Their religion was the Coptic Christianity accepted about 50 AD and adopted as the state religion in Nubia. They were not allowed to kill a royal python or fish in certain rivers. The observation of this law started when a queen of Egypt called Iputu committed abominations by killing her half brother that was the Pharaoh of Egypt as well as her sister. A king of Rome aided and abetted these abominations and God punished them both by turning Iputu into a beautifully colored snake called 'Eke Iputu' while the king of Rome was turned into a fish. Because these involved kings and queens, these animals became royal animals.

Arufo

Chapter Two

The Culture of Igbo People

INTRODUCTION

Upon arrival at the Promised Land without a centralized government, they did not set out to create an empire similar to that of Nubia. They lived in numerous autonomous villages, with strict laws and customs for about 1000 years. The villages were organized into clans while each clan operated their government based on their special believe and ways of worships. Each clan therefore made and enforced codes of conduct commonly referred to as the traditions. In general, the occupation of the people, their traditions as well as their culture suggest strong relationship to the majority of tribes existing in modern day Zambia, Kenya, Southern Sudan, Uganda, Eritrea and Ethiopia, all in North East of Africa. Oral history also suggested that the traditions commonly practiced by these tribes are similar to the practices of the ancient Jewish people as revealed by the Holy Bible (see books of Genesis, Exodus, and Leviticus). After Nigeria was created in 1900 and its attendant independence in 1960, Igbo tradition went into several transformations.

In this Chapter, Ojemba tried to show some of the culture that made the Igbo people unique in their present West African location. The account in this Chapter would explain how the people lived before the advent of Christianity, a factor that had much influence in the transformation of the culture of Igbo people. They have in recent time embraced European Christianity simply because their way of life as well as their belief had always been for one God. In accepting the European Christianity Igbo people renewed their faith in the supremacy of one God, the God of Abraham and Ishmael, their accepted forefathers.

15

IGBO CULTURE IN PERSPECTIVE

Like in the ancient Hebrew kingdoms of Israel and Judah, Igbo people manifest their culture in arts, literature, dance, music, drama, clothing, architecture and other esthetic designs. Story telling, proverbs, idioms, riddles, myths and folklore also play prominent role in the life of the Igbo people. Story telling for instance serves to document actual events, entertain, teach morals and stimulate the imagination of the listener. Some stories also provide commentary on people's lives in a given period. Myths are used to explain events especially the recurrent ones. Proverbs and idioms serve to communicate the wisdom of the past generation. There is a proverb for every situation in life, typically formulated from home experiences and reflections throughout ages.

Igbo proverbs and idioms are central to the propagation of Igbo culture. It is foremost factor in formal conversation and other forms of public speaking. Both proverbs and idioms are devised to make conversions or speeches livelier and enchanting to the listeners or public. Igbo language (Ibo) has in fact been elevated to the status of living art of popular communication. Proverbs and idiom are essential components of kola-nut communion. Idioms are primarily figurative speeches that are coined mostly around animals such as *agu* (lion), *agwo* (snake), etc. Igbo Idioms as well as proverbs require analysis and interpretation that are within the context of a speech or conversation because often times they are very unfamiliar expression especially to young Igbo person or non-Igbo speakers.

Another important aspect of Igbo culture is its religion which embodies every other aspect of Igbo life including the existence of spirits that have power over life and death. They also believe in destiny (*Chi*) and rarely questions misfortunes. In fact, most social symbols are associated with religious faith in spirits (*Okwukwe*). The highest spirit is *Chi-Ukwu* or Chukwu also known as Chineke. Kola-nut is a symbol of life and its communion is life rejuvenating. It is used as immediate tool of appeasement to spirits that guide and protect communities. Igbo children, boys or girls receive circumcision after a given number of days when they were born. Immediately after a child is born, there would be enquiry through spirit high priest (*Ogba-Afa*) of who, among the ancestral spirit was reincarnated. This is because they believed that a person is made up of body, soul and spirit. While body dies, the other two parts transmigrate from body to body. Centuries after the introduction of European Christianity these believes continued to flourish.

Igbo people have Osu and Ohu caste. These are branded individuals or communities that existed due to accident of birth or some misfortunes such as defeat in wars. They become persons of lower class compared to diala. Osu originated from the families set aside to produce priest of shrines or sanctuaries for Igbo spirits such as Ogwugwu, Ihejioku or Amuma. Ohu are domestic slaves sold, bought or voluntarily assigned to people of diala to provide domestic services. Individuals can offer to become domestic servants with the notion of acquiring traditional educations or professionalizing in the areas of the intended masters occupation. Igbos discriminates against each other by reasons of these two caste systems. Igbo residential system follows a patrilineal pattern where sons remain with their father after marriage, while daughters marry to families where they become only partial members. They whiled greater influence where they were born than where they were married to. Marriages can either be monogamous which is prevalent in the 20th Century, but generally Igbo people indulge highly in polygamous marriage arrangements before the advent of European Christianity. Men and women are forbidden to marry within their own patrilineal or matrilineal relatives. In order words parallel or cross cousin marriages are forbidden. Bride prices, which vary from community to community is the essential part of marriage ceremonies.

Igbo alphabets developed by researchers such as F. C. Ogbalu has enable Igbo spoken language to be put in written language also. They invented an accurate calendar of a four-day week which starts on *Afor* and end on *Orie* day. In several Igbo communities, Orie market is the biggest market and day of relaxation for most farmers. Igbo society apparently was an agrarian society. In Igbo calendar, four days make a week, seven weeks make a month, and thirteen months make a year. There are exactly 28 days for each month, with only the last month having 29 days. Mathematically, Igbo people do their counting with *Okwe* and *Mkpisi* while their banking system was more in the nature of savings and loan known as Isusu. In Isusu system, contributions are pooled each week and one person, who has a need, collects.

SOCIALIZATION IN IGBO LAND

In the Igbo homeland, every person-man or woman- had a role assigned to him by the society. He or she learned the ways of the society and the tasks expected of him/she. It is usual for individuals to belong to groups other than family groups within the general society, such as hunters club, Ozo, Nze, Ekpe, Okonko, Oba, and other artisan guilds etc. These various organizations were meant to complement the family role and they exist also to perform certain traditional functions, sometimes in ritualistic ways. Igbo tradition offers two kinds of securities to the people, 'Social and Psychological'. Igbo social organization reflects a close connection between patrilineal groups at various level of segmentation.

In their villages, they were always assured of what to eat, in so far as the village had enough. They were assured of work. When they grow old, the kit and kin would provide for them. That was their social securities. They had to learn a single set of behavior. They know what was expected of them and what to expect from others. They know that when they were married or children are born, or a member of family died, the whole village could participate in an appropriate ceremony to mark the occasion. These were the psychological securities. *Umunna* is a major segment of Igbo villages. These are group of people descended from the same ancestral father, but not of the same mother (*Umunne*). Within a given village, Umunna occupies a specific section and owns common land inherited from the same ancestor. This land is allocated to its members for housing and farming. Umunna is led by a lineage head, the *Okpara*, who is usually its senior member or in some cases, the son of the deceased most senior member of the oldest branch of the lineage. This leader holds "*Ofo*" of the lineage or the representation of lineage guiding spirit. This Okpara performs sacrifices on behalf of the lineage and also carries out important observances for the earth spirit (*Ala*). Thus, Okpara is the Umunna's political and spiritual leader and is a member of village council representing his lineage.

A sub-division of Umunna is the "*Ezi*" or group of Umunna with same surname. It has its realm of rituals, economic and political activities. The head of Ezi is "*Onye is Obi.*" 'Onye is obi' makes sacrifices to more immediate ancestors, allocates land inherited from these immediate ancestors that are not part of Umunna plots. He represents and acts for his constituency during Umunna rituals and members of his constituencies always speaks in smaller or larger gatherings through him. Every person, men or women, devotes one day in an Igbo week to work or serve the needs of this leader. When either the Okpara or Onye is Obi dies, his status is passed to his most senior relative within the relevant subdivision. In many instances, the leadership throne goes to a brother, cousin and in very few occasions, to a son. However, inheritance of personal property, including land bought by individuals from other sources usually passes on from father to sons, under the care of the eldest son. Properties are usually divided according to the number of wives a man has. The first wives' child gets the lion share.

Women do not normally inherit within their families of origin or from their husband. However, any landed property including homes acquired in her name when her husband was alive becomes her personal property. Upon her death, her youngest son takes over the control of such property. Other material properties such as kitchen wares and personal clothing's go to the oldest daughter of deceased woman. Maternal kinship complements these sets of relationship. It is natural to pay homage to the maternal village by every Igbo person. In your maternal home, you are always welcomed and always treated like a son or daughter any time and at any age. At each visit a person usually receives warm hospitality, affectionate and indulgent treatments. Women generally retain rights and relationships with their home communities and visits frequently. All married women within a village often forms a group with well organized and important functions that include religious rites, judicial deliberations, and entertainment, mostly a dancing group. They are usually responsible to organize regulations for grazing goats, sheep and cows within a village.

ORAL COMMUNICATIONS

Igbo people speak *'Ibo'* which is classified as the Niger-Congo language groups. Ibo belong to *'Kwa'* sub family of such language groups. In terms of Igbo people's population, Ibo is the largest linguistic stock of Negro Africa. Olauda Ekwiano was said to have been the pioneer of written language of Ibo. He, in fact, created the first sets of Ibo alphabets as he translated his autobiography (1789), to the language, which he wrote under the pseudonym of Gustavo's Vassa. He was kidnapped from Onicha-Ugbo in the former Benin Kingdom, and sold into slavery to the New World. He lived in England as a free man from where he wrote several articles including his life as Igbo boy. In the 20th century, many writers including the legendary F.C. Ogbalu produced Ibo grammar books and Ibo language had since been studied and used as medium of instruction in schools and colleges in Nigeria and some institutions abroad.

Ibo language has a lot of dialects. The language changes as the location of Igbo people's settlements changed. Going from the extreme south of Ikwere clan of the present day Rivers State of Nigeria to the extreme north of Igbo-Eze at the borders of Benue State, Ibo language has more than 66 variations. In fact sometimes more than a dialect exists in a province (collection of clans). This is perhaps one reason why non-Igbos can hardly learn the language. However, the complexities of Ibo language had made other neighboring languages very simple and Igbo people had learn to speak more than their own vernacular in every environment outside Igbo land. The progress Igbo people made in commerce especially, had been their ability to speak Hausa, Yoruba and other languages spoken by smaller tribes such as Tiv, Igala etc. This has given them edge over other Nigerians in their ability to conduct business in the multiethnic Nigeria. They can communicate and interact very effectively in every tongue in Nigeria and other West African locations.

The complexities of the language are also manifested in various ways items were named. Some items are named differently in different clans and they are generally accepted as Ibo language. Most widely traveled Igbo people understand all of them. A word, *Uri* for instance could mean dance in Owerri province, or one of the tradition cosmetic herbs used by women to decorate their body during festivals. However, Onitsha or Awka person of Igbo origin may call the same word *Uli* having relatively the same meaning. While Igbo people traditionally know who speak what and how, it will be extremely difficult for a non-Igbo person or children born in Diaspora by Igbo parents to know what is what. In fact, several words in Ibo language have more than one meaning, which led some people to suggest that Ibo language is incomplete. Also different words mean the same thing and it is understandable too. Drinking cup for instance, may be called *obele, okuku* or *iko* depending on the settlement. The language has borrowed many words from English since the colonization of African continent.

Ibo language has a few more alphabets than English language. Letters such as n, y, w, k, p, g, b, are combined in various forms to create extra Ibo alphabets such as *nw, kp, gb, kw, gw* etc. This tends to make the language more complex. Many names in Ibo are actually fusions of older original words and phrases. A typical example is green vegetables which is often called "akwukwo nri" which literally means "food leaves." A word often takes on multiple meanings. The word *akwukwo* without a qualifier can mean school, book, paper and/ or education. It may be because printing paper is a product of tree with leaves, collection of paper makes a book and a book is an essential element of school. With a qualifier however, the same akwukwo can take on many forms. One example is "akwukwo ego" which is paper money or bank notes because *"ego"* means money. There are so many examples. Ibo, the language of Igbo people, is taught at all school levels in Igbo land. However, English remains the major language of instruction. In urban centers housing more than Igbo people, the language are mixed with some English words and this is termed "Pidgin English." It makes for easy communication between non-educated and educated Igbo persons as well as non-Igbos within a given community.

PROVERBS AND IDIOMS

Although Igbo people are excellent communicators but the practice of interjecting most sentences with Idiom or Proverbs had always confused most non-Igbos or the younger generation of Igbo people. Conversations are rarely concluded without an interjection of idiomatic expressions or parables (*Ilu*). There is a proverb for every situation in Igbo life. Those who cannot follow conversions because of the added '*Ilu*' are said to be less knowledgeable, while those who can effectively understand and follow conversations are said to be wise. That is, at all times, the elders had the expectations that the young ones could reason out events by themselves and the only responsibility of the elders was to give hints. This they believed would create wisdom because the idioms and proverbs as they are being used serve to communicate the wisdom of the past generations. They are typically formulated through home experiences and reflections throughout ages.

The difference between proverb and idioms is not distinctly clear. Ibo idioms still sounded like proverbs but they are actually figure of speech, which are common in other world languages. The beauty of both Idioms and proverbs are shown when they are written and spoken in Ibo. A phrase, 'Our people said; or my father told; or the elders of our clan said in a proverb . . .' usually start proverbs. However, for purposes of the readership of this book, all the proverbs would be translated into English.

Idioms

a.   A child cannot grow beyond his destiny.
b.   A child cannot pay for his mother's milk.
c.   A clan is like a lizard, if it lost its tail, it soon grew another.
d.   A hunter's dog can suddenly go mad and turn to his master.
e.   A man is judged by his handwork.
f.   A man who has sipped the spirit waters cannot be revived.
g.   A man who will not lend his knife to cut dog meat because that was a taboo but will offer his teeth for the same job.
h.   A proud heart can survive a general failure, because such does not prick its pride.
i.   Age is respected but experience is revered.
j.   An outsider who weeps louder that the bereaved.
k.   Every thing is possible but everything in not expedient.
l.   God will not agree.
m.   He is like small flying bird that so far forgot himself after a heavy meal, and then he challenged his personal spirit or *Chi.*
n.   He tapped my palm trees to death.
o.   He who brings kola brings life.
p.   His worth and not that of his father judge a man.
q.   I cannot find the mouth to tell the story.
r.   I owe them no yam and no cocoyam.
s.   It is like pouring grain of corn into a bag full of holes.
t.   Like a man in a song who had ten wives and not enough soup for his foo foo.
u.   May bullet crack his head?
v.   Never let a handshake pass elbow.
w.   Nothing puzzles God.

x. Opposing him is like a proverbial fly trying to move a dunghill.

y. Proverbs are the palm oil with which words are eaten.

z. The man is as slippery as fish in water.

aa. Those, whose kernels are cracked by their benevolent spirit, should try to be humble.

bb. We are God's flock; sometimes He chooses a young one to eat, and other times, the older ones may be chosen.

cc. We must bale this water now that it's only ankle deep.

dd. We should never fight a fight of blame.

ee. You have put a knife on the thing that held us together and we have fallen apart.

Proverbs

(a) A chick that will grow into a cock can be spotted the very day it hatched

(b) A child on its mother's back does not know that the way is long.

(c) A child's finger is not scalded by a piece of hot yam, which its mother put into its palm

(d) A man who calls his kinsmen to a feast does not do so to save them from starvation.

(e) A person who decided to chase after a chicken in the day light, for him is a constant fall.

(f) An old woman is always uneasy when dry bones are mentioned in the proverb.

(g) As a man danced so the drums were beaten for him.

(h) As dog said if I fall for you and fall for me, it is a play.

(i) As the elders said, if one finger brought oil it soiled the rest.

(j) Eneke, the bird said that since men have learned to shoot without missing, he has learned to fly without perching.

(k) I cannot live on the bank of a river and wash my hand with spittle.

(l) I have climbed *the iroko* tree today; therefore I must come down with as much firewood as I can find.

(m) If a child washed his hands well, he could eat with the kings.

(n) Looking at king's mouth, it may seem he never sucked at his mother's breast.

(o) Madness may indeed depart, but never with all his clamorous train which haunts the eyelid.

(p) Sun will shine on those who stood, before it could reach on those who knelt under them.

(q) The belly does not bulge out only with food and drinks; it might be the abominable disease.

(r) The lizard that jumped from high iroko tree to the ground said he would praise himself if no one else noticed.

(s) Those who gather ant-infested faggot must be prepared for the visit of lizards.

(t) When a man says yes, his personal spirit or *Chi* will always concur.

(u) When a mother cow is chewing grass its young ones watch its mouth.

(v) Whenever I see the dead man's mouth, I see the folly of not eating what one has in one's life.

(w) Whenever you see a toad jumping in broad daylight, then know that someone is after his life.

(x) Who will leave an Ozo feast to attend to poor ritual meals?

(y) You can tell a ripe corn by its looks.

NAMING OF PERSONS AND PLACES

Igbo names are words and phrases used to identify and set people and place apart. Specific names sometimes reflected parent's experiences in life as well as described the circumstances leading to the birth of such child. Such words or phrases can be descriptive adjectives turned into nouns or they may be substantive nouns. Majority of names of Igbo people often has a lot to do with the people's belief in the theory of creation. The understanding was that children are direct gift from God (Seed of Stomach). Certain names are traditionally used to designate men while others are given to women. A number of Igbo names can however be used for either sex. Today, in addition to the traditional names given to children, Christian or baptismal names are common especially among Catholics. This came into existence when the Irish priests ministered the churches in Igbo land. Igbo people were then told that only names of Saints could be used during the baptism. However, Christian influence on first names, which was strong in the early times of colonialism, has began to be less important as some Igbo people began to embrace priesthood. The vernacular names are now being accepted universally as baptismal names or first names.

In the early times, before colonialism, Igbo people did not commonly adopt surnames and last names. People are known by the specific places they came from. However, after colonialism and the introduction of civil service systems, it became necessary to introduce consistent surnames or last names. It was mainly for purposes of taxation and for other administrative exigencies. Once introduced, Igbo people adopted it as they assume that it made for immortality. Succeeding generations used it to venerate the family name as a symbol of permanence. Christianity, in its part, made Igbo people to adopt a threefold pattern of given, middle and surname or family name. Specific motivation for choosing names can be itemized below.

i.   Special relationship between persons can be object for naming children e.g. *Azikiwe*.

ii.   When female children are produced while couples desired at least a male child, they can formulate names such as *Nwanyibunwa or Nkechinyere* etc.

iii.   The people also recognize the limitation imposed by environment for their wishes and desires. Such natural hazards as wars, poverty, death and accidents etc., have influenced Igbo peoples choices of names of their children e.g. *Balogu*.

iv.   Death *(Onwu)* and life *(Ndu)* are known to be mysteries of creation. The people therefore did not waist time to unravel them but expresses their faith in God's domination of such mysteries. Names such as *Agbapuruonwu, Onwudiwe* etc., have therefore been formulated from those mysteries.

v.   Igbo market days and calendar consist of *Afo, Nkwo, Eke and Orie*. Children have been given names of those days especially when they are born in any one of the days. The names could be *Nwafo, Nwankwo, Nweke, and Nworie* for male children, *Mgborie, Mgbafo and Mgbeke* for female children.

vi.   Children are also recognized as precious gift from God almighty and when they are born praise names are often given to them. There is also in recognition that, as precious gift from God, they are much more important than any material wealth or possession. . Example of such names includes *Ibuaku, Nwakaego, and Madukaejiaka* etc.

vii.   Names such as *Chukwumaeze, Chukwuemeka, Nnaemeka* etc., are used to express human faith in God almighty.

viii.   Materials, Rivers, articles of household etc., can be used to name children in Igbo land e.g. *Ofo, Aziza, Orji, Uzuh* etc.

ix.   Children names have been formulated based on the order for which children were born such as *'Okpara'* for the first male children; Ada for the first female child etc. The list below are several other names Igbo parents usually give to their Children:

Females

Akueke, Ahudiya, *Chielo*, Akunna, Ezelagbo, Ezimma, Mgbogo, Nneka, *Nwanyiaeke, Obierika, Mgborie*, Okudo, Akudo, Chinyere, Azunna, *Urekwere, Obianuju, Ihudiya, Ahudiya, Uzoamaka, Udoka, Uzowulu, Ugonna, Uyanwa etc.*

Males

Akuma, Emenike, Duruji, Ezeudu, Ezana, Ibe, Igwilo, Idigo, Madubonwu, Nwoye, Nnaemeka, Obi, Ochuba, Obiako, Odurukwe, Okike, Okafor, Okeke, Okoye, Okagbue, Okonkwo, Ukegbu, Umezuruike etc.

Both Females and Males

Akakamma, Akoma, Ekwefi, Onwuero, Ezeugo, Ezinna, Ikemefuna, Ikezue, Machi, Nwakibeya, Mmadubogwu, Obiajulu, Onwuma, Okika, Ofodile, On-wubiko, Udoka, Udogadi, Onwuero, Umerah, Udenko, Ugomma etc.

A place can also bear names used for the commemoration of a significant clan figure, historical event, or named after towns and cities of the ancient Cush and Nubia where the people originated. For instance, Asaba town across the Niger River was named after the original country of Igbo people, Saba, after one of the sons of Ham, the son of Noah in the bible. Unubi was also named after Nubia, one of the most powerful ancient empires created by the Saba people out of the land of Cushites, who were also the descendants of Ham (*Gen. 10:6–8; Isa. 18:1; Jer. 13:22*).

Igbo villages bear names of mostly the founders. A town can bear a name as follows; *Umuobom, Ndi-Izuogu, Ogwu, Nkerefi etc.* In the first one, *Umu* means children and *Obom* may perhaps be the first settler or the ancestral father of all the inhabitants of the particular place. In the second name, *Ndi* means people of Izuogu probably because it included both his own children and his slaves. The prefix, *Ndi* is mostly used in the settlements created by former slave merchants mostly from *Arochukwu*. Some communities are named descriptively to signify the circumstances of its existence or the terrain and physical features of the specific location such as *Ikpa* and/or *Ikpa-Okoli* etc. *Ikpa* means a free range and probably located by *Okoli* who was the ancestral father or first settler in the location.

EDUCATING IGBO YOUTHS

The educational methods of Igbo people in early times constitute only the informal methods. There were no school buildings but knowledge is transferred from generation to generation through cultural discipline. Igbo people viewed education then as a life long process that includes broad range of other experiences as well as peer relationship and family living. These systems usually occupy more time and often exert powerful influences than does formal schooling, which was introduced in 1800's. The primary purpose of such informal education was to serve the need of the society especially in agriculture, craft and trading process. The emphasis was always on imitation and apprenticeship. Children and young people learn by watching and imitating their elders, usually in work setting. They also learn by trial and error under the guidance of a master *(Oga)* or a specialist. This is a fairly effective way to pass on the accumulated skills and knowledge to the society.

In the 18th Century, elementary, secondary and only later in the 19th century, higher education systems were established based on those in Great Britain. The intention was to provide the colony with clerks, teachers and so forth. Elementary and secondary schools emerged from churches, and these missionary schools were very prominent and continued to play important roles before the Nigerian civil wars of 1960s. Some Igbo people who were able to receive secondary education became such professionals as desired by the civil services system created by the colonial masters. Prominent schools established by the Missionaries include Methodist College at *Uzuakoli,* Holy Ghost College at Owerri, and St Augustine Grammar School at *Nkwere* as well as Iheme Memorial Grammar School at Aro-Ndizuogu etc. The secondary education system that has remained today was designed to give all children a general academic education. The proliferation of secondary and primary schools made the number of people wanting to enter the University swell.

The University education was initiated in the 1960's and they were supposed to provide higher education in all fields. In recent time, admissions to such universities are based on the result of the rigorous joint matriculation examination (JAMB). However, before the coming of the University Education Systems, some tertiary institutions meant to train middle level manpower were established. The prominent ones include; Institute of Management and Technology at Enugu, the Schools of Agriculture *at Igbariam, Umudike and Umuagwo.* There is a Polytechnic at *Nekede* near Owerri as well as a National Root Crop Research Institute also at *Umudike.* Alvan Ikokwu College of Education at Owerri is the foremost advance teacher training college in Igbo land.

University of Nigeria at *Nsukka* was the first indigenous University established after Nigerian Independence. However, in the 1980's and 1990's more universities were established by the government of Nigeria including a University of Technology at Owerri and a University of Agriculture at Umudike. After the creation of states, some states created their university systems. The first of such state Universities was the Rivers State University of Science and Technology at *Nkpolu* followed by the Imo State University at Okigwe, which has since been relocated to Owerri. The former site of the Imo State University was converted to *Abia* State University after the creation of that state from Imo in 1991. The former *Anambra* State University has been changed to Enugu State University also after the creation of Enugu from the old Anambra State.

THE ROLE OF IGBO FAMILY SYSTEM

In West Africa, Igbo was an autonomous nation with distinct culture and tradition until Nigeria was created by the Great Britain. In Nigeria, they are considered as a Tribe; however, they are the second largest ethnic group that makes up Nigeria after the Yoruba tribe. The people believe that they are products of primary or nucleus family (Umunne) as well as polygamous heritage (*Umunna*). Whichever way, they believed that they are blood relatives. It is therefore common for people to refer to each other as brothers and sisters even when they have not known each other previously as long as they speak the same language and their dialect can be identified. The only explanation to justify the universal brotherhood shown by Igbo man could be the fact that they originated from the same ancestors. Some recent writers has postulated that the core Igbo residents from Orlu, Owerri, Okigwe and Umuahia did not come from anywhere but the peripheral Igbos such as the Wawas, the Ikwerres, and Ikais and Onitsha emigrated from various parts of the continent to join them and to become part of them. Why did they openhandedly accept the new Immigrants without question? It is because all came but some came before others.

Igbo family provides its members with protection, companionship, security and socialization. The nuclear family in Igbo land is a subordinate part of extended family, which also consists of nieces, nephews, grand parents and other relatives. Igbo families are patriarchal in structure and the entire structure functions to provide affection and emotional support by and to all its members. Families are responsible for religious training and recreational activities for children in the home as well as socialization with outside children. However, raising children is regarded as the common responsibility of every member of a given village so that, no matter what the relationship between parents, their children still played together and even share their food.

In the late 20th century, extended family system declined in prevalence. The change was associated particularly with increased hardship created by long Hausa-Fulani cum military exploitation of the nation after their defeat in the Biafran wars. Also, increased residential mobility played role in disintegrating the size of the extended family system. Property is usually passed across generation from father to his son, mainly landed properties. The first male child usually, is given the lion share. Women, in some clans, do not inherit any property. Even lands belonging to mothers are always coming from the husbands and after them; the last male child is bequeathed with the property.

IGBO MARRIAGE CUSTOMS

Igbo society encourages marriages in general. The selection of bride by groom was mostly by referral. Love was expected to follow after living together and understanding each other properly. People, especially, relatives made their recommendations based on their own standards and not necessarily that of the groom or the bride. Potential grooms are expected to be providers while the potential brides would be the wealth and property organizers (*Odozi-Aku*). The qualities desired for such grooms were either to own or inherit sufficient property as well as having the physique or the character to maintain, improve or expand such inherited property. He should usually be a good farmer as early Igbo people are mostly agrarian people. They may also be experts in some valued artisans practiced in the society. In order words, jobless and lazy individuals may not be recommended to potential brides. Another important factor that play role in the recommendation, selection and acceptance of both grooms and brides is the family background, including whether such families are Osu, Ohu or any of the forbidden caste of the society. Potentially, both groom and the bride must be free citizens and their families must be seen to be progressive according to the standards of the time. However, the caste group holds the bride or groom to the similar standard but marriage was usually within the system.

The wealth in consideration was usually land, size of yam barn, size of palm plantation and number of domestic animals kept by the family or the extended family. Since marriage is by referral, the ceremony usually consists of several visits to the bride's village or family as well as some rituals. In most clans, at least five visits would be made before a marriage could be considered final. The first visit was for personal introduction to the potential bride herself since most of the time neither her nor him had seen each other before. It is also a visit of enquiry. There had been occasions where parents or the potential bride rejects the suitor's offer and the case was usually closed. However, if the offer were accepted, the second visit would be scheduled where both nuclear families would be introduced. The third visit would be scheduled to set the bride price while the fourth would be to pay a bride price. The final visit would now involve greater number of people on both sides of the village in order to consummate the marriage, as well as to celebrate the union.

The bride price to set depends on the perceived qualities of the bride but in the final analysis, the groom usually pays what he can afford irrespective of the price set and agreed upon. The price gives the recognition required that the two are to be one prior to the final ceremony. No marriage certificate is issued and no church minister or court official is required to proclaim such marriage legal. However, it becomes legal after the payment of the bride price. In each of the visits specified, gallons of palm wine are demanded and obtained. The number of gallons increases with increase in the stage of the visitation. For instance, at the final ceremony, popularly known as *"Igba Nkwu" (Traditional Wedding)* the groom family is to provide enough palm wine to keep the entire village intoxicated for a day or two. Other items are also presented such as snuff, cigarette, food items, goat or other domestic animals. The quality and size of ceremony depends on the clan as well as the wealth and capacity of the groom family. Usually at this final stage, many friends and well-wishers always contribute items to support the groom. This is why they will always intervene in the life of the couple and the woman becomes *"Our Wife"* even though an individual sleeps with her.

Majority of Igbo people lived monogamous relationship; however, polygamous relationships are also accepted. The decision of a type of marriage a person is to enter becomes personal. Usually, barrenness and lack of male children are used as excuses to marry more than one wife at a time. At some other extremes, people practice this because they can afford to do that. Those who can afford to have large families marry many wives. As long as they are wealthy, powerful or famous, many families would naturally allow their daughters to court relationship with such people, they then may eventually end up in being the second, third or fourth wives.

Chapter Three

Sacred Beliefs of Igbo People

INTRODUCTION

This chapter is designed to answer certain questions including: *"What is the people's philosophy of life in general?'* Igbo people believed that religious faith and philosophical understanding are complementary. They combined ethical and supernatural beliefs into a spiritualistic way of life based on the belief that the soul is a prisoner of the body. The soul would be freed at death and reincarnated in a higher or lower form of life, depending on the degree of virtues achieved. Religion therefore, is a way of life while it controlled all aspect of Igbo culture and tradition. In general, Igbo belief system revolved around one God *"Chukwu"* who rule heaven and earth. Their God is omnipotent and omnipresent spirit. They believed that, to reach this mighty spirit, intermediary agents are necessary. One of the greatest agents was the spirit called *"Ala ."* It was said to be the same angel that guided Ishmael to the land of gold called Havilar-Shur at the eastern part of Egypt after he left his father's country. *Ala*, the superior guiding angel of Igbo people was responsible for morality, fertility and general conduct of the people. It was also their belief that more than *Ala*, God almighty appointed several other spirits to work for the general guidance of His creations including *"Chi"* generally accepted as personal spirit of individual Igbo person. Every other spirit reported to *Ala,* who ultimately reports to *Chukwu* who resides in heaven.

ORIGIN OF IGBO RELIGION

The belief system adopted by Igbo people came from their last empire, Nubia. The religion is closely associated with *Coptic Christianity,* an ancient religion

30

adopted in Nubia. Fundamentally, the religion was closely intertwined with every thing else, from the daily task to the most exalted rituals. In the ancient city of Aksum, there was a very powerful emperor called *Ezana* who was converted to Christianity by two Syrians, *Frumentus* and *Adessius*. After accepting the faith, he made it the state religion. While in Aksum, Frumentus played very important role in the emperor's court. After the fall of Aksum and subsequently, Nubia or Cush, the people scattered to various locations in Africa. Igbo people were part of those who left with this belief into their present homeland in West Africa.

Even before the arrival of these two Syrian evangelists, the spiritual practices in Nubia had been strictly *Monotheism*, so was the Igbo practices before the arrival of European doctrines at the shores of Atlantic Ocean. Nubians built several temples dedicating each to various spirits represented in art work, so were the shrines in various Igbo villages representing, *Chi, Amadioha, or Ikenga*. Nubians are said to be related to Earth and they taught the world how to practice life existences and expectations. Igbo people revered the Earth spirit (*Ala*), constantly appease it and assure followers of its closeness to Chukwu. In the general belief of Nubians, God is love and love comes from peoples' heart. Igbo people believed and still believe that Chukwu is love and Ala, Amadioha, Kitikpa etc., have powers of punishment for transgressions and that Chukwu has the ultimate power to forgive sins or transgressions because of His love for humanity.

When Europeans arrived in West Africa in the 19th century AD, they were able to convince the people that Coptic Christianity was equivalent to paganism, especially as they were looking for foothold to colonize the people. How could a people who believe in one indivisible almighty God be pagans? As far as history can tell, Igbo people had always been religious. However, Coptic Christianity may appropriately be described as primitive religion rather the paganism. This is because it lacked the body of sacred scriptures and formal written body of theology equivalent to the Bible of the European Christianity. This is mainly because, before the Europeans arrived, Igbo language, "*Ibo*" have not been developed as such and even till today, the Nubian language writings have not interpreted. Religion in every culture is said to be a way of life. Igbo religion therefore, was an integral piece within the rest of the people's culture. As Christianity was an integral features of the ancient Nubia, Christianity in Igbo land therefore, is older than the arrival of Europeans in West Africa with there theological writings. Since it is so old, it became indigenous religion which was generally misunderstood by the arriving Europeans.

ELEMENTS OF IGBO RELIGIOUS FAITH

Any success or failures of an individual Igbo person are credited to the spirits. A successful hunter for instance, would credit the cooperation of the spirits as much as his own skill. The expression, *"My Chi gave it to me"* was common expression in Igbo land. Artisans including farmers would undertake periodic rituals to insure the fertility of the fields with the same care they gave to the work itself.

Ndimmuo Ala and other lesser angels/spirits are represented by several symbols. *Ofo,* particularly represents *"chi"* and this instrument were usually handed down from generation to generation within each family. Every family therefore has their specific design of *Ofo.* Within each extended family, special houses were erected to place these art objects. Sacrifices meant for the supreme God was offered from the altar of the sanctuaries during or before festivals as well as when misfortune befell on a person within the extended family.

Apart from Ala and Chi, there were several other spirits or lesser angels who may function for protection generally, or for avenging the transgressions of man on earth. While no art objects are used to represent Chukwu, specific objects were used as symbols of those other spirits. These objects are usually housed in common clan or community sanctuaries, the Coptic Church. High priests appointed by the spirits themselves maintain each of the sanctuaries. In each clan or community certain families are assumed to be the representatives of the people in religious sense. It was from these families that high priests of the sanctuaries could be selected. The high priests tend the tabernacles within the sanctuaries from day to day.

It should be noted that Igbo people did not classify Chi, Ala or any other spirit as gods or goddesses. Many recent authors writing about Igbo religion had stated that these are "gods," with a lower case. The use of the phrase, Chukwu-nta (small god) is not common in Igbo language. These deities were rather being referred to as *"Mmuo* (spirits)" or *"Umu-agbara"* (descendant of spirits). Although these spirits were represented by artwork, they were never worshipped as idols. Igbo people believed strongly that the almighty God of heaven (Chukwu) chose these spirits as well as the high priests. In fact, Chineke created every thing in sight including those spirit symbols. Both spirits were said to be the messengers of God, Chukwu or Chineke. People can only approach the almighty Chukwu through the spirits and their immediate messengers, the sanctuary priests. Chukwu appointed them because His work was too great. People offer *"Aja"* sacrifices, not to the spirits but the true God with such spirits and their high priests as intermediaries. People worry the spirits more than they did to Chukwu because they were afraid of Chukwu. They know that Chukwu was everywhere and over all spirits while He remained supreme. The Supreme Being (*Chukwu*) is also known by other names such as *Chineke* (God of Creation), *Obasi dinelu* (God of Heaven), *Amama amachama* (God of Mysteries) etc.

It is the notion of Igbo people that he who does not do the will of God needs to be afraid of his repercussions. They also believed that people were always made to pay for every sin they had committed in their lifetime. They therefore interpreted every misfortune as the punishment for disobedient to God. They also believed that all have sinned and continued to sin and that all fall short of the glory of God. They assumed that God's will was too great to be known by mortals. The general functions of high priests therefore were (a) to interpret the will of God to the people, (b) identify spirits responsible for specific areas of life, (c) communicate with the spirits and ask for atonement when transgressions were committed. If such atonement were ignored, the spirit's anger would then be unleashed on the people not just the transgressor (See Leviticus 5). In this way, every member of the clan becomes the custodian of Igbo culture and traditions. Spirits rule over all natural things that are created by Chineke including water, lands, markets, days or nights etc. Igbo people also believed that creation of the earth was accomplished in four days and that the creation started on Afo day while ending in Orie day. God then rested but on the 8th day He created man to look after His numerous creations.

THE SPIRIT WORLD

All God's creations are classified and specific angels were appointed to rule over them. In Nwabosi clan for instance, while *Ala* remained the earth spirit, "Ndimmuo Ala," there was *Ogwugwu*, the market spirit; *Idemmili*, the spirit of rivers; *Agbara*, the spirit of night and day; *Amadioha*, the spirit of thunder; *Kitikpa*, the spirit of small pox and leprosy; *Agwu*, the spirit of torment etc. Agwu, Kitikpa and Amadioha were assumed to be destructive spirits. They could be used by the *Ala* to avenge pollution or desecration of the land for which she ruled. In general, these spirits controlled the powers of life and death. Like in European Christianity, Igbo people believed that the souls of individuals are converted to spirit when the body died. The spirit however lived forever. Ancestral spirits therefore kept perpetual watch over individual families. The elders therefore, could not eat without calling on the names of their ancestors to come and share what was presented with them. The pouring of libation was the part and parcel of Igbo culture based on the precept that the dead lives on.

The Legend of Ala Spirit[1]

Why Ala spirit was held in higher esteem above all other spirits? Legend had it that she was really the woman ancestor and mother of all Igbo people, probably biblical Hagar, the wife of Abraham. Because she was mother of all, she always had the tendency to forgive man's transgression, especially if people were really sorry for the sins they had committed. However, there were situations when she would allow the vengeance spirits to punish sinners on behalf of the almighty God. When she had not become spirit, she was sent away by Abraham at the wilderness of Beersheba, an angel came and comforted her and gave her certain messages from God, one of which was to guide her children perpetually, life or dead. When she departed this earth, she was sent back as spirit to guide her descendants forever.

IGBO PRAYERS AND COMMUNAL RITES

While direct prayers are not offered to these various spirits, they were however respected as the main link between man and his creator. Igbo people therefore constantly praised the creator whom they also believed to have provided all they owned. The most popular prayer of the people was:

> *Chukwu who made heaven and earth!*
> *The owner of past, present as well as the future!*
> *The commander in chief of both spirit world and mankind!*
> *We pray for good health, life, Children, happiness and good harvest!*
> *We dare not ask for wealth, for when you have given us health and Children,*
> *Wealth was bound to be ours.*
> Chorus: We shall live! Or Isee or Yaa!

Other spirits are sometimes praised but not worshipped. Before offering any kind of sacrifices to God (Chukwu), spirits serving as intermediaries are first awaken with series of eulogies from high priests. Such as;

> *"Dry meat that fills the mouth;*
> *Fire that burn without faggot;*
> *The messenger of great God in heaven;*
> *The spirit who cut man down when his life was sweetest to him;*
> *Please take our message to the almighty God of heaven!!*
> *Pray for us so that He can forgive us for our transgressions."*

Prayers are offered in every public occasion in Igbo land even before the arrival of European Christianity, especially as Kola nut (*Oji*) presentation precedes every occasion. Oji is a cultural symbol that has received the highest attention in Igbo land. Oji is said to be the symbol of life. Igbo kola is always accompanied by palm wine. It is an instrument of Igbo sacramental communion which, when presented must be broken, shared and partaken by every person within a gathering. It precedes prayers and final blessings in every official and unofficial ceremony. Father Jon Ukaegbu[2] has acknowledged in his writings, that the importance of the people's communion in Igbo native rites is analogous to the priest's communion in the modern day churches. In fact Oji is the first thing that is served in every function or ceremony, person or communal agreements, welcoming of visitors to an Igbo home, and settlement of disputes in general. The presentation of kola in each occasion is described as "*Igo Oji.*" Every occasion in Igbo land calls for glorification of God.

In a gathering, Igo Oji becomes a way to bless the crowd, and to ascertain the identity of the attendees. Every section of the community attending such gathering must have a mention. Therefore, before the kola is broken, a person is usually sent to make specific identification of the make-up of the assembly. The blessing of the kola is done by the eldest member of that specific audience. However, where an Eze (Chief) or Nze (titled person) is present, no matter their biological age, it shall be their right to break the kola, bless the gathering and offer libation to the ancestral spirits. Women are not allowed to break kola in a mixed audience; however, women do break the kola when they gather in their usual cultural groupings such as Umuada (women Council), Umuokpu (Higher echelon of Women council), and Alutara di (association of married women). Again, the *oldest member or a Lolo (titled lady) blesses the audience and breaks the kola.* The most prominent ritual specifically associated with Igbo society revolves around the kola nut, the oji. The presentation and breaking of the kola is a symbolic way of honoring the people present, as well as acknowledging spirituality. Kola is considered by the Igbo people to be the food of the gods. It is used both casually on a daily basis and at larger ceremonies where the breaking of the kola nut takes on a more profound significance.

The kola nut, and indeed the kola tree itself, is considered by the Igbo people to be the first tree and fruit on the earth. For this it is particularly revered. The wood from a kola tree, for instance, is never used as firewood, and the nuts are collected in huge quantities and carefully preserved so that it can always be available for spiritual purposes. They are used at every meeting, welcoming, settling of an argument etc. of an Igbo household and community.

REINCARNATION

Igbo people believed that after death, people's souls were reborn or return into consecutive bodies. In order words, human souls are capable of transmigration from body to body. Generally, souls depart the body at death and enter a body at birth. Sometimes they believed that there was improvement from the last life with each reincarnation. Although the ancestors are hovering about, watching over, protecting their individual families, God sometimes select and send back spirits to earth for specific purpose because spirits exist as souls of the dead. Each soul is believed to be sent back to earth as many times as possible and in many forms.

When a child is born, the elders usually enquire from Chief priests of tabernacles of who came to life. The practice is popularly known as "*Igba Afa* (Seer practices)." Often some family members who died would be reported as having come back to life. However, on rare occasions, non-family spirits could come back to a different family. Some spirits returned with all the physical features for which they were identified with, in previous life. Reincarnation is known as a rebirth of spirit which is assumed to never die. The spirit of Ala collects souls, purifies them and returns them to earth at her will. According to this belief, a new personality is developed during each life in the physical world; however some part of the being remains constantly present throughout these successive lives.

The soothsayer or the seer (*Ogba Afa*) often makes a right prediction of a dead person whose spirit came to life as the new baby. However, sometimes they can be in error. When such happened, the child may become sickly and the return to the same or another soothsayer became necessary in order to obtain the right prediction for the identity of the spirit that returned. The returning spirit sometimes made demands on his/her new parents while such demand was usually fulfilled. Sometimes also, the soothsayer or the seer provides dos and don'ts with regards to specific childcare in order that the coming spirit is appeased. The seer may instruct, depending on instructions handed down to him by the spirits that the child abstains from consuming such food materials as pork, snail, or dog meat. If such children are fed with the forbidden ration, the children usually show some serious signs of allergic reactions. In other words, the soothsayer will predict the allergy of specific child under their brief observation.

Some reincarnated spirits may return for purposes of tormenting others, especially their parents. Such parents may not have been nice to them in their previous life. Such return was therefore meant to avenge for ill treatment shown to them specially or for the bad life they led in their previous life. That was why it was not strictly considered evil. They were said to have buried their power of return (*Iyi-Uwa*), beneath the earth and unless such *Iyi-Uwa* is found and destroyed, the child would keep coming and going. In other words, the child would die and the same spirit will come alive with the same notion of leaving at will. Medicine men popularly known as *Dibia* are said to possess special powers to identify Ogbanje, or their *Iyi-Uwa*. When and if *Iyi-Uwa* is identified while the child is still alive, such child will not die again and if he/she died, their spirit will never return again at least in human form.

The Legend of Reincarnation

An Igbo legend had it that the great empress of Saba (Adwa) who ruled between 4th and 7th Century BC was the reincarnate of mother Hagar. It was said that because she had been in the land of Canaan in her previous life, it was easy for her to trace her way back to visit her cousin, King Solomon of Israel. It was also said that the spirit who later returned to life as Solomon was the same angel who brought God's message to Hagar in Beersheba. Both Adwa and Solomon were returned to the earth to rule over the two sections of the Abraham family at the same period. The visit of the queen was to thank her protector spirit in previous life.

AJOHIA (FORBIDDEN FOREST)

Each clan in Igbo land usually set aside a forbidden forest where outcasts, twin babies, and people struck with leprosy and swelling diseases are cast out. Like in the old Hebrew laws, some people are isolated in those forests in order not to spread their diseases which came as punishment for their sins or the sins of their fathers and forefathers against Chukwu. Even after the coming of Europeans, the sacredness of these forests remained. However, these places were finally desecrated when Nigeria invaded Igbo land in the middle to late 1960s. The timbers which had been growing since the beginning of time were carted away by either the invading soldiers or some greedy Igbo collaborators. Fishing in the rivers and streams within the forest were forbidden allowing fishes to grow and multiply indefinitely. The rivers and streams were also desecrated as people started fishing in them. When these forests are cleared, the siltation of major streams and rivers in the entire Igbo land started. The entire environment of Igbo land became polluted physically and spiritually.

FEAST AND FESTIVITIES

Igbo people observe at least three main festivals in each year, mostly to honor *Chineke*. The first of such feasts is *Mmanwu* (ancestral Spirits) festivals to thank God for the maturity of fresh vegetables and fruits of the early season.

This festival is a precursor to the most important feast of New Year and that of harvest. It is also the first feast of the year required to cleanse the society before they prepare for the celebration of new crops. The New Year or new Yam festival that follows is said to be similar to the feast of harvest of the ancient Hebrew tradition and it probably serves the same purpose (Ex. 26:16). In fact most biblical injunctions concerning feasts, festivities and sacrifices in the Old Testament of the holy bible were observed by Igbo people even before the advent of European Christianity.

In the first feast, several Mmanwu are featured. It is said to be the season when spirits came to life for at least three days to honor the chief spirit and Chukwu. Even the messenger spirits such as Ala, Ihejioku, Amadioha, Kitikpa, and Agwu will be appeased for their roles in carrying human messages to God almighty. Each ancestral spirit that came to life in each season can be identified. Women and uninitiated were not expected to come close to the spirits while the spirits perform in various village squares. The spirits were believed to have risen from the belly of earth, the land of the dead, through some ant holes. The leader of the risen spirits would perform certain rituals to cleanse the land at *Ogwugwu* (sanctuary of market spirit) before other spirits could advance into such market. Part of the rituals is to appease the Ogwugwu *Orie* and to allow the celebration of the arrival of new crop before human being can celebrate. The Ogwugwu was expected to communicate with other important spirits that could not come to life and such angels can now pray for fertility, peace, prosperity and forgiveness of human transgressions. Chineke, the God of creation, would forgive, cleans the clan, and bless the people abundantly. These aspects of their belief were what the messengers of European Christianity termed fetish.

Igbo religion, which is often equated to the Coptic Christianity, is not fetish as long as other primitive religions such as Judaism, is not classified so. Even in Catholic faith, the faithful are still praying to God through Virgin Mary, Angel Michael, and other saints (spirits). Very recently, the remains of an Igbo Catholic priest, Father Tansi, who died several years ago in an English Monastery, were brought back to his village in 1994. They said he was canonized, which is interpreted as some step towards attaining saint hood. In fact, by now Igbo Catholics believed that the late father had been admitted to Saint Hood and they believe that praying in his name could work miracles.

The Festival of New Yam

The feast of New Yam, otherwise, Igbo New Year was held every year before the general harvest begins. New Yam could not be harvested or eaten until appropriate sacrifices are made to the almighty Chukwu through the spiritual powers. Men, Women and Children looked forward to the ceremony mainly because it will begin the season of plenty. On the eve of the festival, those who still have yams of the old season usually discard them. The New Year must begin with tasty, fresh yams and not the shriveled and fibrous crops of the previous year. Yam looses water while in storage and usually becomes fibrous just before the new yam comes out. All cooking pots, kitchen wares such as calabash, wooden bowl (*ikpo*), mortar (*ikwe*), and pestle (*odu*) is thoroughly washed before the new crop could touch them. The event usually lasts for two days in many communities. The first day would be for feasting and fellowship, while the second day is usually marked by activities such as wrestling matches at village or market squares. In recent times however, football matches has replaced wrestling in some Igbo communities as the main event of the second day of the festival. Wrestling was said to be savagery and is being opposed by certain sections of Christian communities.

The Legend of New Yam Festival

No one has actually said when this celebration started. It was assumed to have been an injunction given to the people by the almighty Chineke, while their ancestors were still in the land of gold, Havilar, where they were strangers. But indeed, it must have coincided with the discovery of the miracle crop, Yam, which was said to be a revelation from Chukwu. However, in about 10th Century AD, New Yam festival was first celebrated with a lot of fanfare at Meroe in Cush, the one time capital of Unubi-Igbo (Nubia). Before then, it was celebrated privately between families to honor their ancestors. It was the emperor of Unubi-Igbo who decreed that the ceremony became the state affair and must be celebrated with fanfare in all the provinces of his kingdom especially at Meroe. The emperor was indeed a man of God for his deeds were pleasing to Chineke. He encouraged farming and started conferring titles to yam farmers according to their harvest. He proclaimed that a man's worth could only be measured by the size of his yam barn. All that the emperor gave the title became the royal advisers. All the royal advisers including the emperor's household were made to adopt pounded yam as their main meal and no other type of foo-foo was allowed into the royal chamber. The celebration, till today, became the occasion to give thanks to Chukwu through her grace, Ala, as well as Ihejioku through whom Chukwu provided the miracle crop to mankind.

IGBO RELIGIOUS FAITH VS. CHRISTIANITY

Igbo religion controlled the life of the people until late 19th Century when Europeans introduced other brands of Christianity while condemning the people's religious culture and equating it to paganism. The main reason for the

success of Europeans religion in Igbo land was the introduction of the read-
ing of the bible as well as modernizing some rigid codes that had guided people's behaviors for centuries. Igbo religion allowed the seclusion or segrega-
tion of certain individuals called Osu. Although, the Osu caste served as the
chief priests of sanctuaries of worship, they were in fact first to be converted
to European Christianity when the white people came to West Africa.

The early European missionaries built Churches but more than that they
built schools where they taught European culture to the Osu cast mainly and
other free people who accepted their faith. The Osu people were taught how
to read and to write and they were first to be employed in the civil service of
the colonial administration. They became government clerks, interpreters,
court messengers etc. The court messengers were armed and they became the
precursor of paramilitary security unit of the colony. These castes used the
newfound power to avenge centuries of isolation by Igbo people.

The high priests of Igbo religion made no serious attempt to compete evan-
gelically, with European missionaries. The high priest never tried to convert
non-Igbos into their religion. In fact, Igbo people usually obtained their religious teachings from the families rather than from the priests themselves.
Many natural things such as twinning in humans and some diseases considered as abomination in the Igbo religion were disputed by the European evangelists. Thus, these missionaries discouraged such beliefs and convinced the
Osu people (keepers of spirit sanctuaries) particularly, that the spirits would
not harm them if they shaved and accept their brand of religion. Meanwhile,
the missionaries created hospitals and leprosy colonies where the one time
abominable diseases are cured. Twin children were no more abandoned in the
Ajohia. However, most of the actions of the followers of Igbo religions never
had the ability to ask questions as laws and guiding rules were more mystic
than anything else was.

CIRCUMCISION

Before the introduction of the European Christianity, Igbo children were circumcised at approximately eight days after birth (*izu abua* or two Igbo
weeks). It was said to be a covenant they were instructed to keep between
Chukwu and the people. It will be recalled that the bible said that Ishmael for
whom Igbo people claim descendant was circumcised at the age of thirteen.
Thereafter, his father instructed to circumcise all his male children after 8
days of birth. Thus said the Lord; "This is my covenant which you shall keep
between me and you and your descendants after you" (Gen. 17:10). This was
another indication of their link with the Jews.

Circumcision is the procedure that cuts some or the entire foreskin from human genitals. In general, it predates human history. Igbo elders explained this ritual differently. Some said that it was just a form of ritual sacrifices or offering, while many others explained that it was done as health precaution and a means of submission to the will of Chineke. Circumcision is a religious commandment in Judaism and Islam while it is customary in some Coptic, Oriental Orthodox Christian and other Christian churches in Africa. As a covenant however, this ritual is a very personal act as no person has said what the spirits will do if not obeyed. It is probably because the first Church Council in Jerusalem decided that circumcision was not a requirement (Acts 15). Although St. Paul had Timothy circumcised (Acts 16:1–3) but he subsequently wrote letters to Church in Galatia warning them against using this practice to determine membership of their church.

IGBO RELIGIOUS COMMANDMENTS

(i)   *Thou Shall not Kill*
(ii)   *Thou shall not unmask Ancestral spirits;*
(iii) *Thou shall not Mistreat a Stranger;*
(iv)   *Thou shall not kill the royal python*

The most important religious law of Igbo land was not to commit murder of any kind. It was an abomination against the earth spirit and Chukwu to kill generally and a clansman in particular. A person who killed a clansman by accident must flee from that clan into another place where he will stay for several years. After which he performed rituals to cleanse the earth, which he desecrated by his deed. While in exile, the people's property will be confiscated and his compound destroyed, if he had any. If a stranger to the clan committed such act, his home clan should pay for his deeds with another human being and he should perform other rituals to be prescribed by the host clan. These rituals are methods of cleansing the land, which the murderer had polluted with human blood. On the other hand, intentional act of murder was never expected and no laws were made for such incident. Rather, the perpetrator was assumed to be possessed by Agwu (spirit of torment). The contention was that no sound mind and soul could destroy the work of Chineke.

One of the Igbo mystics was the mass return of the ancestral spirits (Mmanwu), once every year especially during the festival preceding the Igbo New Year. However, individual spirits may be called up occasionally and when there was need. They were often used to settle cases, suspend harvest of common tree crops and used to punish transgressors of traditions. They were also used to suspend properties under dispute until substantive cases are determined (interim injunction).

Although women folks were not allowed to stay shoulder to shoulder with the spirits once raised from the ant holes, both men and women are initiated into mysteries of the Mmanwu. Uninitiated were not supposed to come close to Mmanwu unless by accident. Definitely, both initiated and uninitiated were forbidden from unmasking the spirit or to expose the mysteries behind them to the public eyes or in fact to say or do anything that could reduce the immortal prestige of the spirit world. When it happened, it was viewed as serious crime and a lot of sacrifices must be performed to atone the land spirits whose members had been killed. Once a spirit is unmasked, it must not return to earth again i.e. it has been killed.

Igbo people originally were mainly agrarian society, but as their agricultural practices became unsustainable, and as natural resources became scarcer and more expensive, young men and women migrated to other parts of the world. They must however, make annual trips back to the homeland. They in fact became strangers in other lands. Therefore, they learnt to treat strangers with respect especially as they wish to be treated in such other lands they have been. The elders also convinced the youths that that was also part of Chineke's injunction to their ancestors, to treat strangers with respect. This may be similar to those given to Moses on behalf of Israelites. Thus, "You shall neither mistreat a stranger nor oppress him, for you were strangers in the lands of Egypt, said the Lord" (Ex. 22:21).

Igbo people revered and treated royal pythons as if they were a people. It was addressed as a "She" and called "*Eke-Iputu.*" It was allowed to go wherever it wishes, even in people's beds. It ate rats in the houses and sometimes-swallowed chicks or their eggs within the compound. If an Igbo man killed this animal, he usually made sacrifices to atone the mistake. He should also perform burial ceremony such as was done for ordinary human beings. Like in the case of murder, no punishment was prescribed for those who intentionally murdered the Eke-Iputu, because no person thought that people with sound mind could commit such an abomination. In other words, only a lunatic could do such a thing.

The Legend of Cleopatra (Ikputu)

Much of the legend behind this has to do with a Queen called Iputu, who was changed to python because of the seriousness of her sins against Chineke. This Queen had planned with her Greek friends to murder her own sister as well as her stepbrother who was the Pharaoh of Egypt. She committed the sins with active collaboration of a king of Rome. That king also was turned into fish in the great Nile River. That was why the snake became royal python.

Cleopatra really ruled Egypt after she killed Ptolemy XIII, her half brother between 68–30 BC. Although she was famed for her beauty, she was also known for her unscrupulous political dealings. At the age of 16, her mother ensured that she became a co-ruler of greater Egypt left behind by the great emperor of Nubia, Oku-Paleke (Piankhy in most literature). Her unscrupulous dealings, along with adultery especially with foreigners, made her half brother to expel her from the throne and the land respectively. Fleeing to Syria, she met Julius Caesar who restored her as queen. She lived as the mistress of Caesar in Rome until he was assassinated in about 44 BC. Her activities greatly distressed her immediate family. While she was in Rome, her sister attempted to overthrow her with limited success. Cleopatra met Mark Anthony and married him. The warrior moved to Alexandria with Cleopatra where she seized her sister, imprisoned her in Rome and eventually killed her. Their mother died of heartbreak, or so to say.

Chineke punished Cleopatra by sending Angels to help ailing Augustus Caesar (Octavian), to fight both Anthony and the queen in Alexandria. They were defeated and at the brink of such defeat, Mark Anthony committed suicide while the queen chose to die from the bite of an asp (a poisonous snake). After the bite, she went to the tomb she prepared for herself and Anthony and laid. When the Romans entered the palace, they could not find their bodies but saw a snake. After thorough search for their bodies, they concluded that they had changed to animals, snake for the queen and fish for the late emperor of Rome. The tombs were not found until several years later. She was also called Ogbanje, for a normal person could not have combined such beauty she was known for and recklessness she chose to live by. The way and manner she tortured her family baffled Egyptians and all the people of the ancient world. When the Romans announced that she had become a snake, people did not dispute it.

That was why Igbo people chose to revere a beautiful colored python to represent that devil of a woman. God ensured that the killer venom given to all other snakes were not present in the body system of the royal python. In that way, people may torture the woman that committed atrocities in her lifetime, without fear of poisonous snakebite. However, Igbo people believed that such revenge belonged to Chineke and no human being was allowed to do His job for Him.

THE OSU CASTE SYSTEMS

There are people in Igbo land that were made and treated as outcast by the tradition. They are called Osu and Ohu. Both caste systems have limited interaction with free citizens. On the other hand, any contact with Osu by free people that did not involve sacrifices to the spirit sanctuaries where they live, is an abomination. The implication was that the people classified as Osu were those offered to the clan or village sanctuaries. Their duty was to serve the ancestral spirits and to officiate at the sacrificial offering of the people to Chineke. Each village or clan was therefore responsible for the up keep of the Osu caste. Much of their stock came mainly from such offerings to Chukwu. They perform important functions of keeping the sanctuaries for the people and performing the duties of the high priests. They were thus, the intermediaries of such God's messengers as Ogwugwu, *Amuma,* and Agwu etc. They also had some roles to play during the conferment of traditional titles to free citizens (*diala*). People become Osu by one of the following ways:

(a) Persons expelled for violation of traditions could be made to become Ohu or Osu, the caste system.
(b) Those who committed abomination that warranted death sentence may seek sanctuaries from the spirit and once that happens, they will never stop being untouchables, although their lives would be spared.
(c) Those who were expelled from their villages for committing capital crime, but had no other relatives in other clans, who could shelter them, could decide to seek refuge within the sanctuaries of a clan.
(d) If people were oppressed and they ran away to the abodes of spirits, (*alusi*) and said to the spirit, "take me, O spirit, I am willing to become your servant," no man will ever touch them thereafter.

   People who enter the cast for any of the above reasons are free in a sense, yet no power on earth could break their bondage. They are free of men but bonded to the spirit. It was a rigid system where they can only marry their own kind and their generations after them would continue to be Osu. They were restricted from pursuing certain occupations until the advent of European Christianity. An Osu was not allowed to shave and he could not be sheltered or provide shelter to free citizens. In fact, long, tangled, and dirty hair was the major mark of this forbidden caste, wrote Achebe.[2] If free born sheltered or be sheltered by Osu, they become one of them instantly. Osu was indeed a slave to one of the guiding spirits of the clan. He was therefore, a thing set apart, not to be venerated but to be despised and almost spat on. He could not marry a freeborn but from people like him who were bonded to any of the village or clan sanctuaries of guiding spirits.

   The Osu community was large in Igbo land especially since every natural creation of Chineke had its own spirit. There must be families set aside to serve each and every spirit. Although they participated or in fact played major roles in conferment of titles to deserving freeborn, they were never allowed to take any of such titles. Their burial place was the Ajohia. Many members of the caste were first to receive western education in Igbo land. They eventually became well educated and were hired in the colonial administration as clerks and as administrators in many fields. Thus, they started formal contacts with people of non-caste stock. However, it may look like the European Christianity had abolished the system, but it was silently observed till today in many communities even among devote Christians. They no longer carry the mark of the forbidden caste but they had grown into towns and communities. Free people sometimes were reluctant to intermarry with such communities even till today.

INDENTURED SERVANTS IN IGBO LAND

Igbo families had often sent their children, brothers or nephews and nieces to serve another individual as apprentices in various projects, professions and trading purposes. Igbo people believe that this is another form of education and training that usually will not cost the families a whole lot of money. The servants are not paid but must be well taken care of and at a specific number of years, usually 5 to 7, these individuals will graduate and upon good conduct, the masters are suppose to help these servants to set up similar business or profession in another part of the town. Although their services are voluntary, their status is not quite different from that of Ohu.

Ohu, the domestic slaves, can redeem themselves but as long as they remain slaves, their status was not different from those of Osu. Unlike Osu however, the European missionaries made no attempt to change or salvage them. This is mainly because they enjoyed the services of these classes of people. Ohu caste did observe several village activities or socialization because at any venue, their masters still requires their services. Like in the case of Osu, Igbo people were not expected to cause any harm to these people intentionally or otherwise. Ohu castes live among the free citizens, although they may have been bought or captured in wars. They are definitely not allowed to take titles available for free citizens (diala). When they die, their bodies are not sent to forbidden forests. Instead, the masters would provide burial places. Their children may or may not be domestic servants. When their original masters die without selling them, they may become free. If they are sold or willed as a property to other generations, they will continue to be Ohu. Men or women can be bought or sold. Women who bore children for the masters after becoming Ohu would be redeemed. They will become one of the masters' wives. Her children would be free in all respects, including being able to inherit and own properties.

NOTES

1. Legends are part of Ojemba Tales (Igbo Folk Tales). In this chapter four tales were recorded. These legends arose because of the mystic nature of Igbo religious faith. The rituals in Igbo religion are often explained by these tales universally told in Igbo land.

2. Father Jon Ukaegbu is a catholic Priest who has written extensively about the culture of Igbo People including oji communion.

Chapter Four

Igbo Arts and Literature

INTRODUCTION

Igbo artists have developed diverse traditional sculptures (figures and masks), architecture, furniture, pottery, textiles and jewelry. Basket weaving and woodcarving were also prominent. Other materials used in the artwork were clay, earth, stones etc. The forms of representation within each medium vary from relative abstraction to general naturalism. Igbo artists, in the earlier times generally work as specialists, receiving their training from established artists living in the community or wider area. The significant part of Igbo art is the folk tales and oral literatures. Many books have been written to document such stories that were used to convey the right codes of conduct from generation to generation. In this chapter, some elements of Igbo arts and literature were examined.

ORAL LITERATURE

Igbo people had maintained rich and varied oral literature which grew tremendously, since the beginning of Igbo society and continued flourishing till today. The written literature of Igbo people such as '*Ije Odumodu*' and others had always shown a depth to the oral literature, which took variety of forms. Folk tale and riddles are part of Igbo culture that convey acceptable social codes and conducts, while myth and legends teach a belief in the supernaturalism as well as explain the origins and development of states, clans and other important social organizations. Legends and myths are usually regarded as ground in facts. In many instances; they have proved to be extremely accurate accounts of given history of some Igbo people. Folktales, on the other hand, are recognized as fictions. The most famous Igbo folk tales feature tortoise (*mbekwu*), hare (*nwanba*), and spider (*udude*). Some of the tales are formulated to calm the inquisitive minds of children and to entertain the general audience.

Folk Tales

Why Mosquito Goes After One's Ear

Mosquito had asked the ear to marry him, where upon ear fell on the floor in an uncontrollable laughter. "How long do you think you can live?" she asked. "You are already a skeleton." The mosquito went away humiliated and any time he passed the way of ear, he will remind her that he is still alive by making the disturbing sound.

A Quarrel Between Earth and Sky[1]

A child was told how sky withheld rain for seven years until crops withered and the land became so hard that the dead could not be buried. At last, vulture was sent to plead with the sky and to soften his heart with a song of the sufferings of sons of men. Vulture, the earth emissary, sang for mercy as he reached the home of the sky. At last, the sky was moved to pity and he gave the vulture rain wrapped in leaves of cocoyam. But as he flew home, his long talon pierced the leaves and the rain fell, as it had never rained before. And so heavy was the rain on the vulture that he did not return to deliver his message, but flew to a distant land, from where he had espied a fire. When he got there he found that it was a man making a sacrifice to Chineke. He warmed himself in the fire and ate the entrails.

Never Kill a Man Who Had Said Nothing[2]

Mother kite had sent her daughter to bring food. She went and brought back a duckling. "You have done well my daughter," she said. "Tell me, what did the mother of the duckling do when you swooped to carry its child?" The daughter answered, "It said nothing but just walked away." The mother kite said, "My child you must return the duckling because there is something ominous behind that silence." The daughter kite returned the duckling and swooped again on a chick. When she returned the mother asked the same question. The daughter explained that the mother chicken cried, raved and cursed her. The mother kite thanked her and said that they can now eat with assurance that nothing will happen to them. There are numerous stories told in order to answer what and why, to satisfy the curiosity of children. Some include why the shell of a tortoise was rough and looked broken etc.

Oral Igbo story telling is essentially a communal participatory experience. Everybody within a family participates in formal and informal storytelling as interactive oral performances. This is an essential part of traditional Igbo communal life. Basic training in Igbo oral arts and skills is an essential part of children's traditional education on their way to initiation into full-fledged adult hood. Like in many traditional African societies, Igbo people have developed high aesthetic and ethical standards for participating in and judging accomplished oral storytelling performances. Audience members often feel free to interrupt less talented or respected secular performers to suggest improvements or voice criticisms. In Igbo land, storytelling arts are done by professionals, while the most accomplished ones are known as 'Groits, or bards' who have been able to master many complex verbal, musical, and memory skills after years of specialized training.

WRITTEN LITERATURE AND POETRY

In the area of written communications, an impressive body of Igbo literature has been produced. One of such writing was "Omenuko," an Igbo novel written by Mazi Pita Nwanna. Omenuko is a story of an Aro-Igbo man who sold his relatives to earn enough money to recuperate his losses after a mishap at Igwu River on his way to Arochukwu, an ancient Igbo trading post. Such was considered an abomination in those times. It turned out to be adapted from actual event i.e. it was the actual autobiography of *Igwegbe Odum* of *Ndianiche ulo*. Most other literary works of Igbo people described actual events or general ways of living in Igbo land and some were written in English language. *Chukwuemeka Ike, Flora Nwakuche, Chinua Achebe* etc., are the prominent literary giants who described Igbo culture using English language. Achebe particularly, examined Western civilization's influence and threat to traditional values of Igbo people in his early novel "*Things Fall Apart*" (1958). More than 6 million copies of the book have been sold worldwide since it was first published. It has been translated into fifty languages. The Achebe's master piece of work is often compared to the great tragedies of ancient Greek. It was a simple story of a man whose life was dominated by fear and anger. The book was written with remarkable economy and subtle irony. Uniquely rich in Igbo culture which reveal Achebe's awareness of the human qualities common to men of all times and places. "*A man of the people (1966)*," his other novel, was a political satire on corruption in an unnamed African country.

Chinua Achebe was born and raised in Ogidi, one of the centers of Angli-
can Missionary work in Igbo land. He was cited in the London Sunday Times
as one of the "100 Makers of the 20th Century" for defining "A modern
African Literature that was truly African." He therefore made a major contribution to world literature. Chinua Achebe has published novels, short stories,
essays and children play. His volume of poetry, "*Christmas in Biafra*" written during the Biafran war was the joint winner of the commonwealth poetry
prize. Of his novels, '*Arrow of God*' won the 'New Statesman-Jock Campbell' Award, while '*Anthills of the Savanna*' was a finalist for the 1987 Booker
Prize in England. Some of his short stories are collection under a title, '*Girls
at War and other stories*'. Specific titles of the collection include:—"*The
Madman, The Voter, Marriage is a private affair, Akueke, Chike's School
days, The Sacrificial Egg, The Vengeful Creditor, Dead Men's Path, Civil
Peace and Uncle Ben's Choice.*"

Another Igbo prolific writer of literature and novels is *Buchi Emecheta*.
Her first novel, "*In the Ditch*" detailed her experiences growing up as a poor,
single parent in London. '*Second-Class-Citizen*'; '*The Bride Price*' and '*The
Slave Girl*' followed it, which were awarded the 'Jock Campbell' Award for
literatures. Her other novels include, '*The Joy of Motherhood*', '*Destination
Biafra*', '*Naira Power*', '*Double Yoke*', and '*The Rape of Shavi and Kehinde*'
as well as a number of children books and a play. One of her plays, '*A Kind
of Marriage*' was produced on BBC television in London. Another Igbo Poet,
Gabrielle Okara wrote '*The Voice*' which is one of the few African novels to
concentrate exclusively on Igbo characters and values. *Cyprian Ekwensi*
wrote '*Burning Grass*', which has been adopted widely in Nigerian schools
for the study of African literatures.

MASQUERADES AND FACE MASKS

Social themes in Igbo Land are prevalent in masquerade performances. In
these masquerades, animal and human characters, in an appropriate garb assume varieties of roles in demonstrating proper and improper forms of socie-
tal behaviors. Important historical roles are also fulfilled in Igbo art through
its remembrance of some prominent figures and events of the pasts, such as
Ikenga figure at Okigwe Road Roundabout in Owerri town or the fallen soldier at the war museum in Umuahia.

Masks are used for variety of reasons in Igbo land. The shape and forms of
these masks vary according to the specific functions. Some are used to initi-
ate age grades; others are used for funerals, farming ceremonies, marriages,
veneration of ancestors, and messengers carrying specific messages from the

king while most are used as fertility rituals etc. Some personal masks exist such as those carried to represent "*Chi*" personal spirit. Carrying this mask or art object is said to have powers to protect an individual from sudden misfortunes and accidents. In general, the masks represent various spirits and while all are needed to establish harmony among the people and the spirit realm. Igbo masks are sometimes used as a means to instill or teach good morals to younger generations. Some are needed to encourage hard work and generally for uninspired persons to improve on their perception and ideas about personal development. They are also used as an instrument of law and order in Igbo land.

Christianity in general believed that a living person consist of body, soul and spirit. According to New Testament bible, Jesus body died in the cross, his spirit left him and went to the belly of the earth, which is generally referred to as hell. In three days his spirit and soul returned to his body. Thus, He resurrected once more in a complete body, soul and spirit. While On his ascension to heaven, he promised to send Holy Spirit to guide his disciples to continue the great work He initiated. These aspects of Christian believe is not different from the Igbo peoples believe about spirits. While Igbo spirits may never be able to enter their original body just as Jesus did, they can however manifest in other forms, including being reincarnated.

IGBO MUSIC ART

Igbo land had produced magnificent musicians among males and female singers and performers. Among the popular female performers are '*Onyeka Onwenu*', *Christie Essien Igbokwe*, and *Neli Uchendu*. Their song ranged from local high life music's to gospel songs. In the male category, *Osita Osadebe* has been described as the grand father of high life music in Igbo land. Other male performers are *Kabaka, Warrior and late Spud Nathan*. These artists perform in all occasions and are widely known in all Igbo land.

Music is an integral part of daily life in Igbo land. It is also a functional part of a child's natural development. Mothers sing to their babies and introduce these babies to rhythm through rocking them to the beat of music. Moonlight plays and activities consists of singing and drumming as well as other forms of plays that involves music and instruments of music. Igbo children were capable of constructing musical instruments at any organized plays. Until European model schools were established in Igbo land, training of Igbo musician had been an informal affair. Igbo people like most other Africans believed that a person will develop according to his/her own ability and according to what his/her Chi (destiny) prepared for him/her.

Igbo people have a peculiar rhythm of music which consists of drums "*udu*," flute "*opi*," gong "*ogene*," *Igba, Ichaka* and other instruments. The Igbos also has a style of music called "*Ikorodo*" where several instrument are played together while an individual sang. Most of Igbo culture is expressed in music. The udu is considered feminine and is mostly the center piece of women dance group. The ogene are used by all gender in their music but it is usually used to depict the strength and youthfulness of male dancers especially the masquerade groups.

The *Ekwe* is used generally as a musical instrument at coronations, other cultural events, burials and other rituals. It is also used by town criers as a major means of calling for village gathering. The users are trained to change the *Ekwe* sound to reflect the essence of its sounding. Evidently, village people know which sound connotes what event. The various rhythms summon the villagers to the kings' palace (*Obi*), or town square, or to schedule the maintenance of village infrastructure such as roads to common stream (water sources); or to put out fire and other emergencies. *Ogene*, on its part, accompanies dances, songs, religious and secular ceremonies. Its tunes have been developed to produce and transmit messages by some kind of lyric prose. *Igba* is a cylindrical drum covered at one end with animal hide held down tight with fasteners. The player carries it over his shoulders with the help of a shoulder strap and produces the sound by beating on the animal hide with his fingers and drum sticks. Its tunes outside musical performances, gives signal for either good or bad news, such as birth of children or death of an important village person. *Oja*, the flute is a piece of wood designed with a cavity inside, just as the mouth organ or other kinds of flute. It accompanies dances and songs, or can be played as solo by Igbo artists.

BODY PAINTING AND DECORATIONS

Body painting and decorations especially by women, was part of Igbo artistic heritage. Body paints produced from natural herbs such as *Uhie, Edo* (cam wood), *Nzu* (carbonate clay or chalk) etc., are commonly used by Igbo people during festivities. Men are not usually decorated to any extent except as camouflage during hunting or in warfare. Some are rubbed lightly in the skin to perform cosmetic or therapeutic functions. Mostly decorated are women who are of marriage age. *Uri* is another cosmetic herb used both for decorative purposes and for the cure of skin problems caused by measles and chicken pox. Women also wear coiffure made in crest on their forehead. During ceremony also, many women usually dressed up with colored bangles as well as waist beads called *jigida*. They have various artistic styles of hair-do, which the rest of the world had since copied.

All forms of body art used in Igbo land are temporary in nature. Many designs painted on the body are specific to a certain event, or are used to mark a peculiar occasion. Temporary transformation allows an individual to sometimes create a different identity.

IGBO ART: PRESERVATION AND MAINTENANCE

Most of the ancient art works stolen by Europeans in the former Benin Kingdom were the works of *Ikai Igbo* artists inhabiting the Kingdom, West of River Niger delta. Majority of the spirit sanctuaries housed the most exotic artwork of Igbo origins and these were taken away from Asaba area as the people who maintained them were converted to European Christianity. Because it was their production and of important cultural and religious values, Igbo people did not recognize the aesthetic values of these items until in the modern times when such items are exhibited in New York, London and Paris museums. During and after colonization of Igbo land, it is estimated that about three thousand brass, ivory and wooden art objects were consigned to the Western world, mostly from Igbo-Ukwu, Nri, Ajali and Ikai Igbo areas.

Presently, many Igbo states in modern day Nigeria have created cabinet level ministries to oversee the cultural preservations especially for the art culture. It is common to see "Ministry of Sports included with Art and Culture" as sports and gymnastic arts were part of Igbo heritage. Considerable concern of such ministries was both to maintain the traditional artistic forms as well as to encourage the creativity and innovation within the parameters of each art sector. They also maintain dance troupes that compete internationally in art festivals. In Owerri, capital of Igbo State of Imo, the government has also created an art center called *"Mbari"* where both the ancient and modern artwork of Igbo people are exhibited, preserved and maintained.

The earliest sculpture known in Igbo land is from the village of Igbo-Ukwu in Anambra state. In Igbo-Ukwu, the grave of a man of substance dating from 9th century AD was found to contain both chased copper objects and elaborate casting of leaded bronze. Igbo people use several masks to incarnate unspecified spirits of the dead, forming a full range of souls. Mask dancers wore elaborate costumes with their feet and hands covered. The masks of wood or fabric are employed in a variety of dramas to depict social satire, sacred rituals, initiation, burials and public festivals including Christmas and Easter. Some masks appear at only one festival such as Mmanwu and Ekpo-Mgbadike which appears on the harvest festival before the new yam ceremony.

NOTES

1. This tale may either be a way to explain intermittent drought that often come to Igbo land or to explain why the rain was heavier than normal at times.

2. This story is indicating that there is very little to fear from a noise maker. It goes to say that an empty drum makes the loudest noise.

OCCUPATION OF IGBO PEOPLE

OJEMBA STORY

Ukeneme Nwachukwu's children grew to become farmers, traders and black-smiths. As they scattered all over the world, they helped to build cities as trading posts. They made significant contributions in the existence of both modern and ancient kingdoms such as Egypt, Ethiopia, Sudan, Congo Kinshasa, Cameroon and Nigeria. As they moved around Africa, they went with them, their own brand of agriculture consisting of specific and unique crops and animals. They established the agrarian cultures in the Congo Basins and exported such systems to West Africa where they finally made their homeland. They expanded and spoke different dialects, which are collectively called Ibo, a variation of the general Kwa dialect of Negro languages. Some of their ancestors became queens and kings as Chineke had already promised. They ruled Ethiopia and Egypt as strangers while they created Nubia and Nigeria where their influence was greatly felt. History suggested that, instead of defeats in wars, that it was the decline in the fertility of Unubi-Igbo lands that generally motivated their movement to Congo Basin and forest regions of West Africa. The Katanga area of Congo was fertile, so was the Western part of Cameroon Mountains and Plateau areas of modern day Nigeria. These were the motivating factors in the decision to settle in those areas as they arrived in Central and West African regions from the Horn of Africa. They also chose these places because they were close to the emerging empires of Ghana, Mali, Songhay, Benin, Yoruba, and Hausa kingdoms, which provided ready markets for their goods and services.

They developed Igbo land into numerous agrarian settlements until the Europeans sorted them out. The coming of the Europeans started another important phase in their life. The commercial activities were intensified and vigorously pursued as European good enriched their wares. They dominated trades and created both manufacturing and service industries even without established kingdoms. Their commodities had been branded "Igbo made" or "Aba Made" in recognition of their special contributions in enriching the market culture of all Africans. No other ethnic natives can compete or manufacture as Igbo people could.

Arufo

Chapter Five

Agricultural Activities

INTRODUCTION

Igbo people started life as farmers and produced mainly crop commodities including cassava, yam and vegetables. Subsistent and small village agriculture was the pattern. Farms are generally mixed and are family oriented where crops and livestock are produced in interrelated system. All the family members contribute as much labor as was needed to produce crops. Although, farms tend to be small but farmers produce diversity of inter tilled food and fiber products, which was used to sustain a large rural population.

THE FOOD PRODUCTION SYSTEM

The predominant farming systems are based on the shifting cultivation. Such practices were known to be stable and biologically efficient when population was low. They operated effectively where there was sufficient land to allow fallow period to restore soil productivity. Unfortunately, the population of the people grew rapidly while there were significant changes in economy of the area, which necessitated the cultivated areas to expand to marginal lands. The fallow periods therefore were reduced to few years' rotation where it was seven-year rotation. The lands therefore degraded and crop yield declined in recent times. Other practices common in Igbo land was the 'slash and burn' cultivation, which also was sustainable at low population density but very destructive at high population especially when combined with modern tools, and other devices designed to increase production.

YAM: THE KING OF CROPS

While men farmed yam (*Ji*), women produce other crops including cocoy-
ams, beans, spices and vegetables. Even in modern times, yam is still held
as the king of crops in Igbo land. "Yam in fact stood for manliness," wrote
Achebe[1] in his book, 'Things Fall apart.' He further stated "He who can feed
his family on yams from one harvest to another was a great man indeed."
Many yam varieties are farmed in Igbo land. However, they were grouped
into four major categories such as White (*Ji-Ocha*), Red *(Ji-Ona),* Water *(Ji-
Mbana)* and Ordinary *(Ji-anunu).* In general, they are biologically classified
as *Dioscorea spp.*, including *alata and rotundata* species. The water yam
was said to have come from tropical Asia. Igbo ancestors who ruled between
4th Centuries BC and 350 AD in the horn of Africa may have brought the
crop from other regions into Africa. They were said to have helped to domesticate the crop when it was discovered. The white yam was said to be distributed through Ethiopia and Nubian empires inhabited at various times by
Igbo people.

   Yam production was a very exacting business. They are cultivated for their
edible tubers, which grow up to 2.4 m (8 ft), long and may weigh between
10g and 45 kg (100 lb.). The tubers can be roasted, boiled and eaten with oil
and pepper or as yam portage with dry fish or stockfish. It is also pounded to
dough and swallowed with soup thickened by *ogbono, egusi* (melon spp.) or
cocoyam products as well as green and bitter leaf vegetables. For three or four
moons, wrote Achebe; "yam demanded hard work and constant attention
from cockcrow till the chicken went back to roost". The young tendrils were
protected from surface soil temperatures with rings of sisal leaves. As the
rains become heavier, the women planted maize, melon and other vegetables
between yam mounds. The yam crop would then be staked, first with little
sticks *(agbara)* and later with tall and big tree branches *(otugbu)*. Women
weeded the farms three times at definite intervals.

The Legend of Yam

Yam became so important in Igbo life because of the interesting folktale behind it. When the children of Ishmael were driven out of Egypt, they arrived
at a certain forest where the chariots of Pharaohs could not reach. Although
they were safely out of the reach of the invading army, they faced another serious threat to their survival. That threat was hunger and starvation. For several days their children whirled and cried while their parents were helpless for
in several years they had been accustomed to the life of city and plenty in the
civilization. Survival in the forest was therefore strange and new experiences.

However, it was written that they should be forest people. Chukwu took pity on them and sent an angel whose name was Ihejioku to show them the yam that would eventually provide life to them. Although this crop had been growing in the wild but it required the angel, Ihejioku, to point it out to the people.

The angel directed the elders among them to dig out the underground part of luxuriant climbing vines found everywhere in that particular forest. The angel also directed that they roast the tubers and feed to their children. The food was so tasteful that they decided to domesticate the crop. The angel was said to have showed them how to produce the crop and how to care for the crop and the land that produced it. From that time onward, the people never stopped thanking Chineke for their rescue.

PLANTATION AGRICULTURE

The next group of crops Igbo people produce is the 'Oil Palm Tree (*Nkwu*), Raffia Palm (*Ngwo*) and Coconut Palms (*Aku Ohibo*). Each had been discovered to be crop of all round utility. They are of great economic importance because of their fiber, the food, the wine and oil they provide. They also serve other ornamental uses. Palms generally have characteristic growth form; a single, un-branched trunk topped with tuft of fan like or feather like leaves. Researchers noted that about 1400 species occur in tropical Asia; where as only about 120 species were found in Africa. This may suggest that these crops originated from Asia and probably brought to Africa by the ancestors of Igbo people. However, oil palm is now assumed to be a native to West Africa but widely cultivated all over the tropics. Palm oil and coconut oil have become sources of vegetable oil used in making margarine, soap, and other cosmetics and in cooking in Nigeria. The oil palm, classified, as *Elias guineensis* was the major source of revenue for Igbo people before the discovery of petroleum oil. The kernel oil is a commodity needed for various industrial concerns. Raffia palm leaves are used to make roofing mats while bamboo from the tree branches are used for various domestic purposes including staking yam, making chairs and beds, as well as other household products.

Beside the cooking oil, kernel pomade (*udeaku*) and timber from the tree trunk are other important products. All the trees serve important purpose of providing delicious wine to the people. There is up wine, (*Nkwu-elu*), tapped from growing oil palm tree. Another type of wine, less delicious than the up wine could be tapped from the felled trunk. This is known as '*Iti-ala.*' Another delicious wine is that which is tapped from the matured raffia palm. No matter the source, palm wine tapped fresh is very sweet and it becomes sour after some hours of storage. The people who produce these various wines from the trees are known as '*Wine Tapers.*' Tapping of wine is also a man's job in Igbo land.

Palm wine can be fermented and distilled to produce some of the many varieties of dry alcohols. The local or homemade alcohol drink from palm wine is called '*ogogoro.*' Both fresh and other variations of palm wine are used for celebrations especially burial, marriages and other occasions.

FARMING IMPLEMENTS IN RURAL IGBO VILLAGES

Igbo people revolutionized agriculture in West Africa, not only by the introduction of their varieties of crops and breeds of livestock but also introduced iron tools for farming purposes. Igbo neighbors have since adopted metal hoes, cutlasses, sickles and other implements. Almost in every village, there are usually some ironworkers popularly known as blacksmith who produce, maintain and service farm implements for the people. This is a tradition that made historians to suggest that they originated from the ancient world of Saba, Nubia, Meroe as well as Egypt. It was also suggested that the metal hoe culture was evidence of their association with Nok culture, developed in Egypt in the ancient times. Igbo people were therefore part of the Neolithic civilization that revolutionized agriculture and industries worldwide.

NOTE

1. Chinua Achebe's work centers in Igbo Culture and Political Satire mostly dealing with the intricacies of pre-colonial Igbo culture and civilization, as well as the effects of colonialism on African societies.

Chapter Six

Trade and Industries

INTRODUCTION

From the time Igbo ancestors left the horn of Africa, they came in contact with a lot of trading partners including Asians, Europeans and other local inhabitants of empires emerging as time passed. In their homeland, their earliest foreign trading partner was the Portuguese (*Potokiri*). Their occupational successes, both in commerce and agriculture opened doors for creation of urban towns. Aba and Onitsha, two most important commercial towns in Africa were created while international trade was invigorated through the enlargement of some 4-day markets such as Eke-Oha and Nkwo Obosi respectively. Europeans also founded coal and petroleum oil in Igbo land and these became avenue for creating Enugu and Port Harcourt respectively. At Owerre Nchise, the British Petroleum Company, Shell BP, built their camp making once 4-day Eke-Onunwa, a daily market and subsequently small village of Owerre grew into Owerri urban, accommodating people from various areas of Nigeria. The Shell BP labor sites at Oloibiri, Bonny and Ogoni became towns of significance.

EARLY INTERNATIONAL TRADE

Commerce was and continued to be the life wire of Igbo people. The archeological finds at Igbo-Ukwu[1] and other excavation sites produced materials that are very advanced, technologically. It was possible that an International trade existed between Igbo land and the ancient empire of Nubia as early as 9th and 10th centuries AD. At these periods, most of the iron implements and other metal goods including glass beads, bronze art works, elephant tusks and other burial artifacts characteristics of ancient city of Meroe were introduced. However, there were several evidences of metal mining sites in Igbo land at those periods. The expert alloying and casting of several ornamental objects indicate an accumulation of wealth of materials and knowledge from very distant lands. It was either that they acquired the advanced knowledge which prepared some Igbo experts to produce these sophisticated wares or they just exchanged these materials from such distance lands with what they have, including raw minerals from the mining sites. It should be noted that at some period in history, Igbo people occupied the Plateau areas of the present Northern Nigeria where tin and other precious metals are mined. Also farming tools, crops and breed of domestic animals are quite similar to what is obtained at the Northeast of Africa even in modern time.

It was possible that the raw minerals such as tin and silver found in Igbo land was traded for finished products. The elephant tusks, bronze alloying, and other ornamentals stored in burial sites at Nri and Igbo-Ukwu can be regarded as the byproducts of the imports and export trades between Igbo land and her neighbors or with their place of origin. Nri was regarded as the center of learning, and commerce in pre-colonial West African and beyond. Nri was a kingdom of repute because of its control of commercial routes and its opposition to slave trades. Because of this opposition, a lot of Osu (slaves of spirits) and some Ohu (domestic slaves) migrated to Nri where they became free and established numerous businesses.

As late as 1200 to 1800 AD, foreign trading partners of Igbo people were the Portuguese, otherwise known as the Potokiri people. It was the Potokiri people that introduced external slave trade to the area. As early as 1440's, the people would attack each other in order to capture prisoners whom they would sell to the Potokiri. Igbo people sold many of their brothers and sisters who died in such adventure and many Igbo people ended up in Europe and the New World. By the early 1500's, the slave trade was well established in the area. A total of about 8 million West African citizens are estimated to have been sold to slavery to other continents. Of all these people sold, 43% was estimated to be Igbo people since they were taken from Igbo territories of *Opobo, Bonny, Oron, and Calabar*. This may be true since they did not have kingdoms and kings that would have offered some limited protections to the citizens. Ironically, only 23% of the slaves were taken from now famous Slave Coast located at *Badagiri, Benin and Cotonou* because there were kingdoms, which the slave traders had to go through before they transact such business.

As soon as the Atlantic slave trade declined in importance, oil palm products became the trade commodity of choice due to Europe's demand for legitimate commerce. Obliged Igbo people seek new sources of trade and revenue. With time, Palm oil became a highly sought-after commodity by British traders who use the oil as industrial lubricant for the machines of Britain's on-going Industrial Revolution. By 1870, oil palm became the primary export of Igbo people through Port Harcourt and Calabar. Igbo people also tried to trade in cocoa but with limited success.

NETWORK OF DISTRIBUTIVE TRADE

In modern times, the main center for distributive trade in Igbo land is Onitsha town. It is in the present Anambra State of Nigeria by the Niger River valley. In 1966, the longest Road Bridge in the country connects it to Asaba. All the consumer items, including industrial products are traded here. It was site for teachers college for women and leper colony. The city is also the resident of the Obi of Onitsha. The entire town is a block of market. The main center of trade however, is the *Ochanja* main market established in 1927. It was the site of *Nkwo Ukwu*, an original four-day market near the bank of River Niger. When the palm kernel trade developed into international trade, the market became daily affair. The influx of strangers who came to help the white traders started establishing settlements, thus the creation of urbanization.

Onitsha became an important trading port for the Royal Niger Company in the mid 1850's with trade in palm kernels and other cash crops booming around the river port. Igbo people from the hinter land as well as the European traders were drawn to Onitsha. After a bridge was built in 1965 across the River Niger, trade soared between the eastern and western parts of Nigeria. This made Onitsha the strategic gateway for trade between Igbo people and the rest of the world. Industries started emerging in the town. Products like textiles, beer, mineral water, shoes, lumber, tires, nails and printed publications were produced by Igbo people living at Onitsha.

Aba is another commercial city in Igbo land. In contrast to any other town in West Africa, Aba has the highest number of small scale industries. It is noted for its famous *Ariaria* Market. It is densely populated and has a high ratio of artisans in its population. The town is known for marketing its home made products such as dresses, bags, and shoes which are known as "*Igbo Made*" or Aba Made. In Aba, there are numerous shopping centers beside the famous market. Major malls are at Eke-Onunwa market between Cameroon and market roads. The city is quit suited as the confluence of business hub because of its location. It lies at the intersection of roads from Port Harcourt, Owerri, Umuahia, Ikot Ekpene, and Ikot Abasi (Opobo). Aba was a traditional market town for the Igbo people before the establishment of a British military post in 1901. In 1915, British constructed the railroad from Port Harcourt to Aba and the town assumed the responsibility of becoming a major collection point for agricultural produce.

Majority of the small-scale industries is located at Aba, which had been described as the "*Taiwan of Africa.*" These consumer goods manufactured and used in West Africa are popularly known as 'Igbo made' or 'Aba made.' Goods manufactured at Aba are distributed through Onitsha market. Aba is one of the largest towns in Igbo land. It is part of Abia State on the Aba River. A railroad and number of roads serve Aba. It is the important manufacturing center for consumer goods including textile mills, soap, pharmaceuticals etc. There are also numerous shoes, mineral water and beer industries established around the city. In 1929, Aba was the site of the women's war also called 'Aba riot.' Aba riot started when the British officials imposed high taxes at the background of low returns on the people goods especially, the oil palm resources. The women of the area rose and demonstrated against such taxation. Government troops were sent in and approximately 50 women were killed in the conflict.

Other smaller towns within Igbo land or Biafra also play roles in promoting business and commerce around the nation of Igbo people. Igbo businesses all over the world is estimated to worth more that a trillion naira per annum. There is more wealth distribution among Igbo people than any other group or tribe in Nigeria. Igbo business men and women are increasingly expanding their frontiers within Africa and the rest of the world. In all business pursuit there is always Igbo spirit which embodies hard work, honesty and thrift or self discipline.

INDUSTRIALIZATION PROCESS AND URBANIZATION

As early as 1300's, Igbo people started mechanical processing and extraction of oil from both the fruit and the nut of palm tree for export. Palm oil trade became the backbone of the economy of Igbo people especially after the slave trade was abolished. They have also been able to create textile mills at Aba and at Onitsha. There were cement factories at *Nkalagu* while asbestos roofing materials and sewage products are being manufactured at *Emene* near Enugu. Also rampant in Igbo land are various kinds of brewing industries. All kinds of alcoholic drinks are being manufactured including beer, stout and malt drinks in various locations of Igbo land. Saw milling industries are also rampant and this sector of the economy contributes significantly to the growth of some cities and provinces. Other small consumer goods such as food processing are being operated.

Although industries are scattered all over Igbo land, but Aba became the industrial hub center of Igbo people probably because of its closeness to Port Harcourt and Calabar, two ports that served Igbo people. Enugu, the original capital of Igbo people was a major coal mining and trade center. It lies at the southeastern foot of Udi hills. It was founded in 1909 after coal deposits were discovered near Elugwu Ngwo. It became the administrative center after the railroad to Port Harcourt was completed in 1912. It was a regional capital of Eastern Nigeria and subsequently that of Biafra. Manufacturing in Enugu is conducted in the suburbs since it was administrative headquarters. It is the home of the 'Institute of Management and Technology.'

Port Harcourt is presently the capital of Rivers State since 1970 and was the leading port of the country. It is a road and rail hub and a major industrial center especially after the discovery of petroleum oil. Igbo people used the port facilities to export palm oil, petroleum, coal, and other palm products. Industries located in the area include saw milling, auto assembly, food canning, flour milling, tobacco processing, and the manufacture of rubber, glass, enamelware, paints, bicycles, furniture and soap. The port was established in 1915 to serve Eastern Nigeria, the Igbo territory. Located in the city are the 'University of Science and Technology' (1971), and 'University of Port Harcourt (1975).' In Onne town, a suburb of Port Harcourt, urea and ammonia fertilizer products are being manufactured to serve Nigeria farmers and export market. Also, at Onne liquefied natural gas is being manufactured although mined at Oloibiri.

TRANSPORT SERVICES

Because of the nature of the commercial activities of Igbo people, they tend to be the major providers of road transport services to all parts of West Africa and Cameroon. From Ochanja Market Park in Onitsha, and Aba Main Park at Milverton Avenue, people can travel to Yaunde in Cameroon, to Freetown in Sierra Leone, to Cotonou in Togo, to Accra in Ghana etc. They also control interstate transport services within Nigeria. Popular carriers include *'Izu Chukwu', 'Chidi Ebere', ABC transport, Oriental lines* as well as the most popular *Ekene Dili Chukwu*. These transports Services would take people and their goods to all nooks and crannies of Nigeria and West Africa. There are domestic airports at Enugu and Owerri as well as an international airport at Port Harcourt. However, Igbo people depend heavily on its network of roads. In the late 1970's, expressway was built to link Enugu to all major town southward, including Okigwe, Umuahia, and Aba while ending at Port Harcourt.

HOW THEY CONDUCT BUSINESS

Igbo people are known to be fair and just because all opinions are counted in business. They are generally ambitious, industrious, energetic and unacquainted with idleness. The people were all habituated to labor from early childhood and they are competitive, progressive, and proud. They tend to succeed in their entire quest because the extended family assured it. In trading posts, they usually lived together and protected each other from external hostilities. In Northern Nigerian cities of Kano, Kaduna, Sokoto, Zaria etc., Igbo people settled in Sabo Ngari i.e. 'Land of Strangers.' Their level of decency and honesty in business was very high and they always seemed to be socially more civilized than the average citizens of their host community in West Africa. All these qualities attracted both envy and jealousy.

By their commercial prowess and organizational ingenuity, they were instrumental in the creation of all known trading centers in West Africa at least. However, despite their efforts, they were still being considered as strangers in most of those places. In Lagos Nigeria, they created the famous 'Alaba Electronic Market', Oshodi Central Market and many other outlets around the Island. They controlled the import and export trades and were responsible for the distribution of goods and services throughout the length and breath of Nigeria. They have settled in all sections of the country, and in any major cities and even minor ones. In other West African cities, Igbo people controlled significant percentage of trading rights because of their business acumen.

NOTE

1. Dr. Isichie listed the mining sites in her writings (History of Igbo People).

POLITICAL PHILOSOPHY OF IGBO PEOPLE

OJEMBA STORY

Igbo philosophy included a belief that leaders are made only in heaven. Kings or emperors could only emerge by the will of Chineke. Igbo people therefore had always waited on the lord for guidance in choosing suitable and acceptable leaders whom the people would honor with absolute respect; thus, the connotations, Chukwuma-Eze, Eze-Chukwu, Chukwu-ga-ekwu etc. Miracles and sometimes, mystic signs were always expected before confirmation of a chosen leader. When it was not Chineke's time, Igbo people had been known to stay hundreds of years without a central leader or appropriate central government. It has sometimes led to the speculation that; Igbo people are leaderless (Igbo Enwe Eze). When and if a leader emerged, he/she is expected to rule with fear of God, otherwise when they die, Chineke would prevent their spirit from reincarnating. Each leader would actually bear the spirit of one of the departed ones. Because of this believe, leadership tussles are rare in Igbo land when a leader emerged.

In about 50 AD, a chosen leader, emperor Oku-Paleke (Piankhy) who ruled greater Nubia was said to have borne the spirit of Menelik 1. He was selected by God to lead his people but he spent more time expanding his territory beyond the lands of his people, that he angered Chineke. Although, two of his descendants, Ptolemy XIII and Iputu (Cleopatra), ruled in several places including Egypt, the disastrous decline of the empire afterwards as well as premature death of Akeha, Iputu and Ptolemy, his children, were attributed to his disobedient of Chineke's injunctions.

In the 20th Century, Chukwu also chose a man called Nnamdi Azikiwe (Zik) to lead Igbo people in their homeland. As a sign of his emergence, there was eclipse of the sun as well as other wonders of Chineke. Many more things had happened including his knowledge, which was equated to that of spirit and his ability to survive despite many attempts on his life by the white people. In short, his emergence was miraculous as no historian had been able to state, which, his extended families were and how he was able to go to white mans country as early as he did. He battled the British people single handedly to liberate his people. The British eventually gave him the opportunity to create all Igbo nation in 1952. His successes however, went into his head, that he demanded the entire Nigeria from them. Eight years after, he achieved it but because it was his personal ambition and not what he was called to do, Nigeria of his dream crumbled and his people were massacred in the same country he labored greatly to create. When his people finally wanted to do Chineke's Will it was too late and millions of Igbo children were sacrificed because of Zik's disobedient.

In doing more than Chineke's directives by expanding their territory far and wide, they caused and accepted adulteration of their people's beliefs and culture. Other cultures were allowed to infuse into Igbo traditions, which was antithesis to Igbo heritage. By over-stretching also, they lost and compromised significant portions of their people's territory. In these two instances, where the chosen ones misinterpreted their calling while replacing Chineke's Will by their personal desires, the entire Igbo people suffered. In fact, they were bruised in Nigeria between 1965–1970, in the same way they were battered in Unubi-Igbo (Nubia) in the ancient times. However, Chukwu loved the people and had always provided ways and means by which they survive such disasters. If and when He had not chosen a leader for them, Chukwu also provided means for the people to preserve and maintain their cultural values in small but well organized village settlements. He had directed in such situations that the people's authority be delegated to the "Ofo-Custodians" (Obu-Ofo). Ofo was the principal symbol of Chi as well as the personal, family and collective village ancestral spirits.

Arufo

Chapter Seven

Igbo Leadership Systems

INTRODUCTION

There was no historical record of a single individual before Zik who had been elected, nominated or appointed to rule Igbo people since they entered the Promised Land in about 500 BC. However, in absence of such kingly figure for generality of the people, Igbo people had been able to maintain law and order, while preserving their cultural heritage in the homeland. They have scattered to all parts of Africa, created settlements of Igbo people in many places other than the homeland. In these settlements including their homeland, they constituted the authorities to look up to, and had created the capacity to adapt while holding tight to their heritage. In villages and collection thereof, there were traditional rulers whom they have not been able to classify as kings or emperors. Each however, takes the title of *Eze-ala*, after the famous king of Aksum in the ancient times.

The scramble for Africa by major European powers, and subsequently, the colonization of Africans, resulted to the creation of modern nation states in all parts, including West Africa. After such creations, no ethnic group to that effect maintained a region wide feudal system or what could be described as uniform state or empire of one people. The existing feudal lords were stripped of their powers and where a single monarch reigned, Europeans appointed multiples of them in the name of indirect rule. From the Hausa Kingdom of the ancient time came numerous emirates with each emirate having an emir. In the Yoruba west, Ooni of Ife and Alafin of Oyo were stripped of their powers and many more Obas were appointed in various Yoruba locations. It was therefore not strange for Igbo people to have several Eze's especially, after the colonization of the people by the British.

PROLIFERATION OF KINGSHIP IN IGBO LAND

Like in several other ethnic African nations, Igbo people have numerous Eze-ala including *'Obi of Onitsha, Igwe of Orlu, Abrakata of Umunze'* as well as so many others that are not well known beyond the borders of their community. All are supposed to have influence all over Igbo land but the jurisdiction of each is restricted to specific communities. Igwe performs traditional rites of Orlu people while Obi is traditional custodian of Onitsha town. Several Eze-alas were in fact appointed to all autonomous communities, no matter how small they are. In other words, Igbo people have more than 5000 traditional kings beside political and military leaders in the current dispensation. However, since Igbo people have not been able to have a single Eze-ala, they have not been able also to organize a nation state in the modern sense as they did in Nubia or Cush.

One reason why such nation had previously not been created even before colonization may have been the fact that many sub groups of Igbo people entered the homeland at different periods in history. Ngwa sub tribe was said to have come to the place before others while the most current entrant was the Ikai Igbos inhabiting the Western Delta regions of River Niger. Each sub tribe such as Wawa, Mbaise, Bende, Olu, Ijekebee etc., acquired several traditions that may be conspicuously absent from several others. Their system of government indicates no separation between state and religion and no such separation between culture and religion also. All those Eze-alas were therefore the custodians of the culture, tradition and religion of specific clans of people. It would have been inappropriate to have a single king since clan laws slightly differed. There was also very little common interest that would have warranted the formation of a single entity called Igbo nation. However, as opportunities for such common interest arose, such as regulation of international trade and general commerce, new system of government emerged.

THE STATUS OF TRADITIONAL IGBO LEADERSHIP

The system of governance in Igbo land before the colonization has been described as "Imperial Nubian style of Democracy." Decision-making was generally by consensus, which enabled every age grade to participate in the governance of his or her clan. Just like in ancient Nubia, all clans were free and self-governing. The saying, "Igbo Enwe Eze" gave a very wrong impression that the people are leaderless. On the contrary, they have chosen and produced remarkable leaders whom they believed were crowned only in heaven.

In fact, no group would be able to exist peacefully without leadership that is as effective as Igbo leaders had been over the years.

In recent times, Igbo people have both traditional and political leaders whereas the separation of state and religion was observed in modern society. While the selection of the traditional ones are based on the religious belief held in ancient times, the selection of people on the political category was based on the laws of the modern nation state of Nigeria. The traditional kings (Eze-ala) are the protectors of, and custodians of traditions and culture. In short, they oversee the maintenance of law and order in their individual settings since such traditions vary from clan to clan.

Most communities cannot give the history of how a certain family came to produce the Eze of their community. In many others, due to economic reasons, the original traditional stools have changed to other families and people still accepted that as the will of Chineke. No leader however, was above the law and traditional leaders did not go about amending the traditional laws or repealing any sections of it. In short, the laws of the land before creation of Nigeria were unwritten but vivid in mind of the people.

Politically, Igbo people are very democratic and egalitarian. The system of governance involves several layers of organized assembly including the 'High Council of Elders" at the apex of such many organizations. Governance was much more diffused than anywhere else in West Africa was. They maintained strict republican leadership with representatives drawn from several organization, communities and villages. Many historians have described the system as novel democracy, and the people, as true democrats respectively. However, historically it was the same system operated in Nubia in the ancient times and in the land of Judah before King Saul. Speaking at the 1979 Ahiajoku lecture series,[1] Professor Michael Echeruo, the first Vice Chancellor of Imo State University, suggested "Igbos as a people lack the monolithic cohesiveness characteristics of a people with long history of communal interaction."

In another angle, a British historian named Sylvia Leith-Ross who was commissioned to study Igbo culture soon after the women revolt of 1929–1936 stated, "Igbo people are true democrats." As early as the 8th century AD, some Arab traders found Igbo land to be a highly organized society with developed traditional towns such as Ajali, Aguleri etc., as well as well organized commerce, trading network and settlements governed democratically. Even in their settlements outside Igbo land, the people developed sophisticated society that was involved in trade and other human endeavors. They had rule of law that was the envy of the Europeans who traded with them. "The people are seldom unjust", noted some European traders, while they observed that there was complete security in their settlements all over West Africa.

THE PEOPLE'S GOVERNMENT SYSTEM

Igbo people possess three main levels of leadership groups, although several organizations, especially secret societies, were often involved. The supreme body was the *'Council of Elders'* that performed executive as well as judicial functions. They take executive decisions on important issues as well as act as court to settle disputes. Other groups such as *'Age Grade'* and *'Umuada'* (Women Council) complement the roles of the Elder's council. On an individual village, the council of elders was made up of all the custodians of *Ofo* or family heads while the chairmen of such councils usually were the oldest members of such assembly. All the chairmen from different villages formed the town council while the clan council members were the Eze's of all such autonomous communities.

Where there are titled men, (*Nze and Ozo*), they usually became permanent members of the assembly and even chair some sessions irrespective of their biological age. A community Eze was usually an initiated member of Ozo society or any other secret society prevalent in such community. The Elders Council made laws to preserve the customs and traditions of Igbo people mainly. They however could legislate on issues concerning inter communal relationships as well as regulated the life of the people to ensure that *"Taboos"* are not committed. Basic laws of the land were also religious laws and the people were expected to obey them religiously. Since they were religious laws, all offenders were regarded as having transgressed against Chineke (supreme God). Punishment for transgression therefore, came as atonement in form of sacrifices to Chukwu. When such atonement was not forth coming, the transgressor was usually excommunicated from the general society and sometimes exiled to other clans or communities.

It should be noted that there were no prison houses; however, lawbreakers may be asked to pay fines of various amounts depending on the community and depending on the nature of offence. They may also loose some rights and privileges available to other members of the community. In the extreme case, individuals may be banished from the community and all their life worth confiscated. Many books including "Things Fall Apart" recorded significant information on how and what constituted high crimes or misdemeanors in Igbo community in the ancient times. Throughout history there were also no records of imprisonment in the Nubian empire. However, as a human society, it was likely that lawbreakers existed in Nubia and the exile system as well as atonement rituals would have been used as corrective punishments of such lawbreakers.

AGE GRADE AND WOMEN COUNCIL (Umuada)

Age Grade

The entire Igbo villages are usually broken down into compartment of groups and organizations based on their ages. The oldest member of each compartment led each group and these are called age grades. Their functions were really to keep busy, avoid troubles, learn several traditional arts including dances, as well as provide avenues for educating the youths. It also provided easy access to obtain human resources needed in times of national or community emergencies. Elections are rarely held in such groups. However, most of their leaders were selected based on the biological age differences or for the fact that a particular individual had distinguished him/herself in competitive sports such as wrestling. Sometimes, those who had led the people successfully in wars could be honored with more leadership responsibilities. Even those who had succeeded in commercial enterprises, or had the largest size of yam barn compared to others have assumed the leadership responsibilities, politically. In fact, any person that made any contribution considered significant in the community or personal sacrifices can ascend the ladder of leadership irrespective of his/her biological age. This leads to a popular saying (Idiom): *Nwata Kwo Aka Osoro Ogaranya Riwe Nri*. Literally, this is saying that a child with a clean hand can eat with his/her elders.

Umuada group or Women Council

A typical example of Nubian culture prevalent in Igbo land is the involvement of women in the society governance. Another important group of leaders in the traditional sense were the *Umuada* (women council). These are the women born in a given village or community, who were also married within and outside the community. Immediately a person was married, she would be initiated into the society by performing certain rites. She then took her rightful place in the council, which was also compartmentalized according to age. The most senior members of the council functioned in similar fashion as the appeal court in modern times. They review the decisions of all groups within their paternal community especially such decisions that remained under dispute. Their responsibility was to review such issues to the benefit of the village or the community. Their decisions were expected to be just, fair and probably, final. However, they are rarely called upon except on extreme emergencies. In all village functions including burials, this council was usually accorded the highest honor after the titled men. Their opinion and decisions on matters were always respected.

The British colonial masters did not take into account the leadership role Igbo people accorded to their women. However, they insisted on taxing women whom they have not accorded any type of representation in their system of government. Aba riot or women's revolt became the most significant event that occurred in Nigerian history during colonialism. Many writers observed that after the revolt, the colonial administration realized that differences existed between cultures of different tribes put together as Nigeria. In other words British knew very little about Igbo people whom they have ruled for about three decades. After the riot or revolt, they took measures to promote Igbo studies. They requested specific studies through their District Officers (DO) of the culture of Igbo people. The British appointed Mr. M. Green, an anthropologist as well as a British historian called Ms. S. Leith Ross to study and present a report as part of enquiry on the revolt. Basically these individuals should study the unwritten history of Igbo people and to pay specific attention to the roles of women in Igbo Society. They discovered that it was comparable to Nubian culture and that women play similar roles on all spheres of Igbo life as men do.

INITIATION AND CONFERMENT OF TRADITIONAL TITLES

One of the major leadership groups of Igbo people was titled men. There were several societies that confer recognizable titles to the men of Igbo land. There were therefore, several varieties of such titles available for taking. Some of such societies include *Ezeji, Okonko, Ekpe* and *Ozo* etc. In recent times, Chieftaincy titles, belonging to no specific society, had been conferred on some personalities. Most titled men belonged to the cabinet of individual traditional Eze-ala (King). The general symbol of all titles, except the Chieftaincy, was red cap, and ankle rope or string of a title. All the societies and their members were respected in all Igbo land irrespective of where they were initiated. Ozo, however, was the most prestigious of all the societies. Not all of these titles are available for taking in all sub-tribes of Igbo nation. Ezeji for instance, was popular among the people of Umuahia and Bende division while people of Arochukwu; Abriba, Item, Ohafia etc mostly took Okonko and Ekpe. Ozo, on the other hand, was very popular among the communities in the old Orlu and Aguata divisions of Imo and Anambra States of Nigeria. Aro-people that are scattered all over Igbo land were not allowed to take certain titles.

OZO TITLE AND RED CAP CHIEFS

Like all Igbo society titles, the symbol of membership of the prestigious Ozo society was a redcap generally and ankle rope for members of certain rank. A person who had been conferred with the title was called *Nze*. There were several levels of Igbo titles and four steps in Nwabosi and other surrounding clans known as *Onozie, Ajaro, Ikeji* and *Ichi* respectively. Those who were initiated into the beginning steps were referred to as *Nze-Nta* (small Nze), while those who have moved beyond that first step were called *Nze-Ukwu* (big Nze). In the four stage ranking, only Onozie was considered as Nze-nta while the three others were called big Nze.

The highest class of the title in the old Orlu Division or Aguata was 'Ichi,' which was also not available for taking in many communities because of the nature and process of initiation. Ichi holder was considered as the spiritual commander-in-chief or a generalist. Usually, rivalries and petty jealousies may have hindered so many people from achieving this title. There had been many stories of where people, who were initiated into the rank, did not live to enjoy their special privileges or command the society as expected. So, either out of fear or cautions, people had carefully avoided that level of initiation no matter how rich they may have been. Among people of the same rank, seniority is also recognized. That is, no matter the biological age differences, those who were initiated first became seniors and they deserves the right and privileges of senior members of the society.

In the Onozie classification (Nze-nta), the holder could only wear the redcap to identify himself as a member of Ozo society. However, in most gathering, in absence of non-members of the society (*Akpukpaa*), the Onozie holder became the messenger of all the assembly. The services they could render included breaking and distribution of items of entertainment including the kola nut. The rank of Onozie was used to establish the citizenship of an individual within a community. Immediately a person was admitted, every other person would now recognize that he was actually a son of the soil (*Nwafo*). Among the qualifications for this initial entry into the Ozo society was the ability for the applicant to recite oral history of his specific ancestors. He would also be able to give in a chronological order, his seventh ancestral generations including his immediate father and grandfathers. The reason was that outcast (Osu or Ohu) as well as strangers (*Mbiarambia*) was prohibited from taking any of the titles of a clan.

It would constitute an abomination if these titles were conferred to any of the above group in any clan. If however, it was done in an error or deceit, sacrifices would be offered to the ancestors while the head of the Ozo council would loose his leadership position but he remained as a member of the society. Therefore screening became a very rigorous affair and time consuming, especially if non-of the parents or grandparents of the applicant was a member of the Ozo society. There is therefore a waiting period where also the characters of the individual could be verified. This is to avoid initiating a criminal into the society. If either of the applicants parents were Nze, his citizenship had therefore been established while a shorter waiting period mainly to verify his character would be applied. There are other conditions to be met, including verifying if and how the applicant's parents or grandparents were buried and if appropriate burial rites were done. After Onozie rank, all other ranks could be attained without hitches depending on the applicants. In all the ceremonies during the initiation, all the animals used, chicken, goat, cow etc., and all the kola-nuts must be of Igbo breed and variety respectively.

IGBO LEADERSHIP UP TO NIGERIAN INDEPENDENCE

Because of the agitation spearheaded by Igbo nationalists, British tried to compromise by granting Eastern Nigerian (Igbo area) self-government in 1952. As Eastern protectorate, the region was divided into 20 provinces with provincial administrators at the helm of affairs. Enugu was established as the capital of the Igbo dominated protectorate. A bicameral parliamentary system of government was established with executive branch consisting of Premier, Governor and ministers, who as a matter of fact were elected members of the house of assembly. The two body of the legislature includes the house of chiefs and the general assembly. The members of the house of chiefs were nominated from among the traditional rulers some of who were appointed by the British. However, traditional stools like '*Amanyarabo, Obi, Igwe, Jaja* etc. were accorded the right of permanent membership of house of chiefs. Few other community Ezes were nominated to boost the number in the house of chiefs. The assembly of chiefs was supposed to be the superior house to that of general assembly. The members of the general assembly were elected from individual constituencies within the provinces.

The elected premiers of the region who were also the executive head of the regional government were Dr. M. I. Okpara, Dr. Eyo Ita, and Dr. Nnamdi Azikiwe at different times from 1952 to 1966. Dr. Akanu Ibiam was the regional governor for those periods. In 1960, the legendary Zik was appointed the governor general of Nigeria and subsequently, the President of the federal republic in 1963. In 1966, both the regional and Federal governments were toppled by the military. The then Lt. Colonel Emeka Odumegwu Ojukwu became the military governor of Igbo region, which he subsequently declared as a republic of Biafra in May of 1967.

LEADERSHIP OF BALKANIZED IGBO
LAND AFTER THE CIVIL WAR

After the civil war, Biafra land was first divided into three states; East Central, Rivers, and Cross River States. The division of Biafra land into three states aided in disaffection in the war effort. Particularly significant was that the places removed from the Igbo heartland were the areas containing oil wells and other mineral resources including natural gas. Igbo people in those areas denied their heritage, probably in order not to be discriminated against. In the East Central State proper, one Mr. Ukpabi Asika was appointed from Lagos to be the administrator of the now, land locked state. He was a postgraduate student at the University of Ibadan when the war broke out. He and few others were either voluntarily or otherwise trapped in the Western Nigeria. The Lagos junta sorted out these individuals and used them to form the government of the East Central State.

At the end of the war in 1970, Mr. Asika collected handful of these people and returned to Enugu the former Capital of Biafra. Because of the circumstances surrounding their appointments, the administration of Mr. Asika became so unpopular. One reason was that the people could not immediately trust the decisions of the Nigerian junta and secondly, because the people were not given chance to decide on who should look after their affairs. Another reason for the unpopularity was also because members of that administration were those whom the people considered to be betrayers of the people of Biafra. The people therefore viewed Mr. Asika's administration as improper and illegal while so many people refused appointment in his government. Even the legendary Zik disapproved of him and his government, although, it was said that Zik actually went to Lagos and arranged for the end of war.

When Mr. Asika was removed few months after his appointment, Colonel Anthony Ochefu, a native of Idoma land of Benue State, was appointed to govern the state. Ochefu's tribe is the immediate neighbor and possibly, relatives of Igbo people. For that and many other reasons, the army officer was sympathetic to the cause of Igbo people, although he participated, as adjunct general of Nigerian army, to fight Biafra. His sympathy to the people of East Central State brought problems to him and to the people of the state. It seemed that he was not fulfilling the agenda of the military against Igbo people as demanded in Lagos. He set out to repair and rebuild structures destroyed during the war including roads and schools in urban centers at least. What they actually wanted him to do was to further punish the people, which he was not doing. Few months after his appointment, Colonel Ochefu was recalled to Lagos, stripped of his army rank and removed from the army.

Brigadier Murtala Mohammed never obliged the nation an explanation for his actions in this respect.

Atom Kpera, a corrupt army colonel who later plundered his own native state of Benue, was appointed to replace Ochefu as the military governor of the land locked state. He was probably directed to ensure that the faith of the people they were unable to seal in active war was final sealed. People like Wole Shoinka suggested that the entire nation of Igbo be subjected to become nothing more than farmers, when BBC interviewed him on the treatment meted to the people. So it became obvious that the agenda to continue to deprive Igbo people was a collective one, not just of the Nigerian military. Atom Kpera therefore collaborated with some infidels and greedy politicians to exploit the war torn people. Their resources were carted away to Benue State and he, Mr. Kpera, was rewarded with another promotion to the rank of Brigadier.

When Murtala Mohammed was assassinated in February of 1976, the East Central State was further split into Anambra and Imo States with Enugu and Owerri as their capitals respectively. Fortunately, two navy officers of Igbo origin were selected to govern the two states. Navy Commodore Ndubuisi Kanu from Ovim Isikwuato was the military governor of Imo while Navy Captain Alison Madueke from Inyi near Achi, was the governor of Anambra. Both tried, to the limits of their resources, to create administrative and social structures as well as motivating the people's participation through self-help efforts. The people became mobilized in order to rebuild the war damages. Although, the psychological war was still raging, Onitsha, which was burnt to ashes during the war, as well as Aba, which was a war sector for a period of 11 months, was all refurbished to some extent. When General Obasanjo, the head of state of Nigeria, visited these states, he became marveled at the rate of reconstruction going on without the input of the central government. He was particularly startled at Onitsha, which he knew was burnt to ashes because he commanded the army that destroyed the place in 1969. Beside bad roads, the place was more bustling than anywhere else in Nigeria was and there were very few signs that the place was a war zone.

IGBO LEADERSHIP LEADING TO NIGERIAN 2ND REPUBLIC

In 1978, as new constitution was fashioned for Nigeria and people were allowed to form political parties after long years of military rule (1966–1978). Igbo people resurrected the NCNC but called it Nigerian Peoples Party (NPP). After all, they were the people who actually wanted Nigeria among all the major tribes. The constitution was fashioned on the style of United States system and the legendary Zik again led his people. After the election, NPP won the two Igbo Central States, in addition to their one time ancestral home in Plateau State. The party also had significant showings in all the states in central Nigeria including Niger State where Zik was born. For four years, Zik boys, Dee Sam Mbakwe (Imo) and Mr. Jim Nwobodo (Anambra) transformed their various places while creating new industries along with some social structures including rural electrification's. They built new schools including institutions of higher learning, which was previously, the domain of the Federal Government. Onitsha and Aba became the center of international trade in Nigeria. Igbo people started to take pride in their existence and they started playing leadership role in many spheres of life in Nigeria except in the military.

FURTHER STATE CREATION WITHOUT EQUITY

In December 1983, soon after Alhaji Shehu Shagari and Dr. Alexander Ekwueme were reelected for another four years, they were overthrown in a coup led by Maj. General Mohammed Buhari. The ruling military council named some civilians to occupy many key positions and said it had seized power to end corruption and solve the economic crisis heightened by the dramatic drop in oil revenues. Nigerian economic problems continued, however, and Buhari was overthrown in August of 1985 in a bloodless coup led by the army chief of staff, General Ibrahim Babangida. He started the effort of economic restructuring while promising the return to civilian rule by January 1993 under new federal constitution he was to fashion out in 1989. Local elections under a two-party system were held in 1990. In an unsuccessful effort to ease continuing religious and ethnic tensions, nine new states were created in August 1991. Igbo states were further split into Abia (Umuahia), Enugu (Enugu), Anambra (Awka), and Imo (Owerri). State elections were held in December, while the national assembly elections were held in July of 1992. Four separate individuals were elected in Igbo land as the Governors. They were Dr. Chukwuemeka Ezeife (Anambra), Dr. Ogbonnaya Onu (Abia), Dr. Okwesilieze Nwodo (Enugu) and Nze Evans Enwerem (Imo). Widespread fraud was alleged during the September 1992 presidential primaries.

In October, the government suspended political activities pending an investigation, and in November, Babangida announced that the transfer to civilian rule would be delayed until August 1993. In June the National Electoral Commission headed by Dr. Humphrey Nwosu, an Igbo person and political science professor at the University of Nigeria Nsukka conducted an election, which was annulled by the military. In 1994, the acclaimed winner of that inconclusive presidential election, Chief Moshood Abiola was arrested for declaring himself president of Nigeria.

In May of the same year, a constitutional conference was convened to discuss the development of a democratic government but progress was slowed down by personal ambition of Gen. Sanni Abacha, the then minister of defense who overthrew the head of interim government Ernest Shonikan. Not contempt with being the military head of state, Sanni Abacha wanted to perpetuate himself as life president of Nigeria. Apparently, in 1998 both Abacha and Abiola died mysteriously. Abubakar, a kin to Babangida was horridly promoted to the rank of general in the Nigerian Army, before he assumed the position of the head of state. He remained the head of state until election was held when Dr. Ekwueme's political organization, "People Democratic Party, (PDP)" produced the majority members in the national assembly and appointed one of their leaders, Olusegun Obasanjo, as the President.

After the June 12 fiasco of 1993, and the subsequent overthrow of the interim government, the military looked for avenues to keep relevant and to justify their prolonged stay in government. They have failed to stem corruption and in fact, Nigeria came to add to its vocabulary "419" which signifies a criminal code dealing with advance fee fraud. Short-lived *Novo Rich* created by various economic scams including money laundering and drug pushing became the order of the day. The military boys were conspicuously identified with these activities. The military kept people busy with bogus return to civil rule agenda. Instead of facing reality, the people started clamoring for new local governments and new states to be carved out of the existing ones. In 1996, Nigeria was further split into 36 irrelevant states, where non-can effectively fends for itself without the oil money from Eastern States and Igbo dominated Delta state. Igbo land retained Port Harcourt area as new Rivers State without the people of Yenegoa while Abakaliki, Afikpo and Ohaozara areas became a state called Ebonyi.

NOTE

1. *Lecture series directed towards understanding of Igbo Culture and Civilization. It was inaugurated on Friday,* November 30, 1979, with a lecture "A matter of identity-Ahamefule" *delivered by Professor Michael Echeruo, the first Vice Chancellor of Imo State University.*

Chapter Eight

Colonization and Decolonization
of Igbo People

INTRODUCTION

A British Empire builder called Sir George Goldie formed the United African Company (UAC) during the European scramble for Africa. UAC later became a commercial concern designed to promote the British influence in the Niger River regions. In 1886, the British parliament granted a charter to Goldie's enterprise, renaming UAC to become the 'Royal Niger Company.' The company obtained extensive administrative powers in the area they later named Nigeria. Sir Goldie became the governor of the Company in 1895. In 1900, the company's territory passed under the direct British colonial control. The Royal Niger Company accomplished much of the British acquisition of Nigeria. Other European countries at the conference of Berlin recognized the British claims to the Niger basins in 1885. Earlier, in 1884, the colony and the protectorate of Nigeria were established with Sir Frederick Lugard as the governor-general. Colonial rule itself brought some inherent problems that would ultimately lead to independence and subsequent conflicts among the ethnic groups brought together by the British. Igbo nation was one of the groups that came under the southern protectorate.

Nigeria gained independence in 1960 through the efforts of Zik and other Igbo nationalist. The new country was composed of three regions—Northern, Western and Eastern—each of which was represented in the central government. In 1963, it proclaimed itself a republic and established the fourth region—Midwest. With the help of British especially angered by potential loss of the oil revenue engineered by Igbo people, the North continued to dominate the country politically. However, there was no significant progress in the economic and social sectors. Friction developed between the southern people including Igbo people and the Northern people. Unfortunately, Igbo people taught that because they fought and drove the British out of Nigeria, the country was theirs. They were therefore caught in the middle of ethnic envy and jealousy.

IGBO PEOPLE AS PARTNERS TO BRITISH COLONIAL AGENTS

In 1914, the southern and northern Niger protectorates were united or amalgamated to become a country called Nigeria. Before the two sides of Nigeria were united, Igbo people had been everywhere in the northern side as well as Lagos protectorate, trading and doing other human activities. In the northern part, they were responsible for the success of the indirect rule because they acted as intermediaries between the Europeans and the local population. They spoke the languages of various natives as well as the English, the language of the colonial masters.

Igbo People were used by the British to further their territorial interest. Igbo people were employed in the new civil service system. In fact, Igbo indigenes constituted more that 70% of all public work forces in Northern Nigeria[1] in the 19th and early 20th centuries. They became court clerks, court messengers (*Kotma*), interpreters (*Nwelekebe*), especially as they were able to speak other local languages besides there own language. Their children populated the newly established British type school systems while they eventually became highly educated in the British values, culture and religions. Most educated people attracted white and blue-collar jobs in colonial administration. When the West African Frontier Force was created to aid the Royal Army in the world wars, the relatively educated Igbo people were drafted while they formed the backbone of the force.

EFFECT OF COLONIZATION ON IGBO CULTURAL VALUES

Upon the unification of different West African kingdoms to form Nigeria, the British tampered with various cultures especially Igbo culture including their representative administrative system, destroying a democracy model that had worked for centuries. The colonialists designed the indirect rule system, which necessitated appointment of chiefs where they did not exist previously. They created the chiefdoms for purposes of taxation, which was unknown in Igbo land. While Igbo people settled in all parts of Nigeria, driven by their entrepreneur skills and proclaiming nationalism, other ethnic people held tight to their traditional values. In fact, no other tribe embraced Nigeria as Igbo people did. And non-of those tribes lost so much of their cultural values as Igbo people did. Igbo people threw their religion and its doctrines overboard and accepted entirely the various shades of European religion. Many Christian religious sects took it upon themselves to destroy the original sanctuaries of worship of Igbo people. They allowed the British scavengers to steal all the symbols of their spirits. It however brought what may be considered modernization and urbanization. Their commercial activities intensified and many new industries were established.

AGITATION FOR NIGERIAN INDEPENDENCE

It took several years and the leadership of Zik for Igbo people to realize that they were not equal partners with British people in Nigeria. In 1945 however, the agitation for independence started. These agitation, ironically, were spearheaded by Igbo nationalist including Mbonu Ojike, Zik, Okpara etc. One of the highlights of the agitation was a general strike called by the coal miners at Enugu, the Igbo capital city. Train services were disrupted to the Northern parts of Nigeria. Movements of general goods including food commodities were restricted as a result. Food became scarce in all parts of Nigeria, particularly in the Northern provinces. Realizing that the situation may soon render Nigeria ungovernable, the district office representing colonial administration blamed Igbo people while whipping the sentiments of other tribes against Igbo people. Igbo people were subsequently attacked in their homes and their market stalls at Jos, Kaduna, Kano and Zaria.

On March of 1953, when these Igbo nationalist in the House of Representatives at Lagos tabled a motion for Nigeria independence for 1956, the British angered by such motion engineered the Northern members to make counter motion of "Independence for Nigeria as soon as possible." This counter motion, which was defeated, was designed to give British the opportunity to continue to colonize the country. Because of the defeat of this motion Igbo people again were attacked in all parts of Northern Nigeria.

IGBO PEOPLE AND NCNC (A POLITICAL PARTY)

One of the effects of colonialism on Igbo people was the loss of their system of government that worked for them for several centuries. Another was bringing them from Cameroon into West Africa because of the important role they played in formation of Nigeria. They however, did not forget their origin and when they were allowed to form political parties in colonial

Nigeria, they organized a party known as "National Council for Nigeria and Cameroon (NCNC)." In the same way other parties were formed including the 'Action Group (AG) and Northern Peoples Congress (NPC)." The AG and NPC were more or less tribal affiliations for the Yoruba West and the Hausa Fulani North, respectively. NCNC, on the other hand was a more nationalistic political grouping of people from all over the country. Various ethnic groups including *Cameroon, Ibibio, Nupe, Chamba, Tiv, Idoma, Igala, Ijaw, Efik, and Calabari* etc., belonged to NCNC probably because of their cultural similarities. The founder of the party was *Herbert Macaulay* who in recent time was honored with his face in one of the Nigeria currencies or bank note. Some of the party leaders were non-Igbos including Professor Eyo Ita from Ibibio tribe, *Margaret Ekpo* from Calabari also included are some prominent individuals from both South West such as *Adelebu* (The Penklemesi) and the Middle Belt regions of Northern Nigeria such as *Joseph Tarka*. However, important Igbo leaders who wielded very strong influence in NCNC were *Alvan Ikokwu, Zik, M. I. Okpara, Nwafo Orizu, and Mbonu Ojike* etc.

NCNC therefore, was a broad-based political organization, which had more national outlook than the NPC or the AG. It was probably branded Igbo peoples party by those other organizations, which were actually jealous or envious of their wide appeal. Political intolerance became rampant as interests differed among the rival parties. Individual voters from Yoruba speaking as well as Hausa-Fulani speaking areas were forcibly prevented from joining the NCNC. After independence, the NPC who controlled the central government developed a strategy of reducing the size and spread of NCNC and even the AG, including using the national resources to create additional region in the south and ceding part of East to Cameroon Republic. They went further to promise an autonomous state to the Riverrine areas of the East, whose citizens later started to foment troubles, which were never nipped by the Alhaji Abubakar's government. A regional status was granted to Mid West. Although, NPC actively proposed and supported policies that divided the south, they used the entire national might to subdue agitation for the creation of Middle Belt region in the North.

The attitude of the Yoruba members of AG, including outright and open intimidation of Yoruba members of NCNC ensured the permanent disunity of the south, which the NPC fully exploited. The demonstration of this fact was the NCNC winning of the 1954 election in Western Nigeria under the leadership of Zik. However, after the meeting of 'Egbe Omo Oduduwa' (Yoruba cultural organization), several Yoruba speaking NCNC legislators suddenly resigned their membership of NCNC, thus, "Crossing Carpet" to AG. These move effectively prevented Zik from becoming the first premier of Western

Nigeria. This was not only the beginning but also the height of tribalism in Nigerian politics.

NIGERIAN CRISIS AND THE PRICE OF TRIBALISM

After the 1954 carpet crossing fiasco in the Western Region, the leaders of NCNC lost faith in the southern unity. Soon after independence therefore, the NCNC formed an alliance with the NPC to form the central government. The AG then became the opposition party in the house of parliament. The leader of the AG, Chief Obafemi Awolowo then became the opposition leader. Before he left to lead the opposition in Lagos, Chief Awolowo relinquished his premiership to his assistant, Dr. Ladoko Akintola. Although he was in Lagos, Chief Awolowo tried to control the government of western region remotely. However, Dr. Akintola, who effectively took over as the premier resigned his membership of AG to form his own party that later aligned with the NPC.

The new alliance became "Nigerian National Alliance" (NNA). Dr. Akintola justified it by claiming that he wanted to move the Yoruba ethnic group to the main stream of Nigerian politics contrary to the opposition ideology of Chief Awolowo. In 1965 however, the 'New National Democratic Party (NNDP)' of Dr. Akintola won the regional elections amidst the accusation of rigging by the AG members and leadership. However, Akintola eventually formed the government but violence ensued afterwards. There were riots and bloodshed throughout the Western Region, which soon became known as the "Wild West." People, mostly the Yoruba's were killed indiscriminately. Arson was committed while law and order completely broke down. War was unofficially declared between the supporters of Awolowo and Akintola. The notorious slogan, "Operation Weh-tie" became the mob sentence for any known supporters of the opposing party. Human bodies were strewn in the streets throughout the region.

THE FIRST MILITARY COUP AND IGBO CONNECTION

The national Prime Minister, Alhaji Abubakar Tafawa Balewa was not seen to have done enough to contain the riot and protect human life. Life generally came to a halt in Ibadan and other areas of the Western Nigeria. The President, Zik, was on vacation on the Caribbean Islands while the West was burning. In the absence of any significant actions from these two leaders to restore law and order, some members of the armed forces carried out the first military coup in Nigeria on January 15, 1966. The coup was code named "Exercise Damissa II. The primary aim of the coup, the people were told, was to restore law and order and to subsequently rid the nation of all corruption and nepotism. The coup attempt failed, having been suppressed in its final stages by forces loyal to the Federal government. However, the civil authority surrendered their government to the military, voluntarily after the death of several government functionaries including the Prime Minister, the Premier of Northern Region, Sir Ahmadu Bello, and the Finance Minister, Mr. Okotiebo. In fact, the entire leadership of the "NNA alliance" was completely decimated.

Although, Major General John Thomas Aguiyi-Ironsi, the GOC of Nigerian Army, took over the government, the coup was still regarded as having failed. It was in fact, mismanaged from onset and such mismanagement almost caused the demise of the five-year-old country. Exercise Damissa II was planned and executed by the famous or infamous five majors mainly to stop bloodshed in the Western Nigeria, and only secondarily to sweep out the corruption that had eaten deep into the fabrics of the new country. In fact, that coup was a Yoruba coup if it should be ascribed to any ethnic group in Nigeria. Ironically however, the coup leader was Major Chukwuma Nzeogwu who was born and bred in Kaduna, the capital of Northern Nigeria. His parents however, were Igbo people who originated from Okpanam community near Agbo in the former Benin Kingdom. The basic error was the sparing of politicians within the NCNC and AG political organizations. In fact, no Igbo born politician was killed in the coup and therefore, it was termed Igbo coup even by the Yoruba people whose riot the coup was meant to stop. Non-Igbos including the Yoruba people interpreted the coup as a design by the Igbo people to dominate the rest of the tribes. The assumption of power by General JTU Ironsi, an Igbo officer from Umuahia, did not help matters.

GENOCIDE AND MASS RETURN TO HOMELAND

Although, General Ironsi moved to restore law and order in the West, he was killed less than six months after his assumption of office as head of state of Nigeria. Hausa-Fulani soldiers carried out his assassination mainly, as a revenge for the assassination of the NNA leaders in the civilian dispensation. However, he was accused of proposing and instituting a unitary government, a system that was fully exploited by the Hausa-Fulani oligarchy several years after. The July 29, 1966 counter coup was very catastrophic to Igbos generally. Northern civilians and soldiers massacred Igbo people living in the West and North. In fact, some of the January coup plotters who were Igbos, such as, Major Don Okafor and Chris Anuforo were abducted from their prison cells in Western Nigeria and killed by their northern colleagues under the nose of the Yoruba people. The counter coup therefore caused major ethnic friction especially between the Hausa/Fulani in the North and the Igbos. During these upheavals, many Igbo people living outside eastern Nigeria, military or civilians were killed and consequently, many fled to their homeland in the East.

Although the coup had occurred because of the Yoruba crisis, many Igbo people living in the North regarded it as a victory to their cause, especially as Ironsi emerged as the head of state. They therefore became arrogant in their joy. They demonstrated carrying banners and placards with slogans that tended to jeer at the death of the northern leaders. The real fact however, was that the Yoruba soldiers who, in not carrying through their assignment of eliminating Igbo politicians as was planned, had fumbled badly. After the assassination of the head of state, about 100,000 other people of Eastern Nigerian origin were massacred in cold blood. A novelist, Buchi Emecheta recorded that, "Some who escaped death by Hausa mob died of trekking to the homeland; significant percentage of women who reached Enugu alive were without one breast." In fact a lot of people were maimed. In the Western Yoruba part, things were even more chaotic. But whereas in the North the massacre was carried out in the open, in the west, it was done discretely. People who had the remotest connection with Igbo land started to disappear even in Lagos. Many dead bodies of people from the East were found floating along the Lagos creek.

NOTE

1. Most of these Information can be found at the Civil Service Archives, Museum of colonial administration Lagos Nigeria.

Chapter Nine

The Declaration of Biafra

INTRODUCTION

The 1966 coup organized by five majors led by Chukwuma Nzeogwu of the Nigerian Army was branded an Igbo coup. Other tribes started what could be described as retaliatory actions by killing and maiming Igbos everywhere in the territorial Nigeria. Frightened Igbo refugees from all corners of Nigeria streamed to the East on daily basis. The newly appointed head of Nigeria, Lt. Colonel Yakubu Gowon made only a frail effort to stop the Igbo massacre through a half-hearted speech. The real fact was that he had no power to actually stop the mayhem. The entire world watched while a nation of people was being exterminated. Not even the former colonial master, Britain, had the courage to reprimand Nigeria. However, the head of state of Ghana, General Ankra invited both Gowon and Emeka Ojukwu, two former pals on the opposite divide, for a peace conference. When the peace conference failed, Igbo people demanded from their leaders the declaration of Igbo Republic. As soon as the republic of Biafra was declared few countries including Gabon, Haiti, Cote d'Ivoire, Tanzania and Zambia accorded the new republic, recognition. Nigeria responded by declaring war on the new republic as well as blockading the new state to starve the people. Other nations such as France, Israel, Rhodesia and South Africa provided covert military assistance to Biafra. Island of Sao Tome and Principe became the center of humanitarian relief effort. Biafra set up an overseas office at Lisbon, where also its currency was printed. The secession ended in a catastrophe in 1970 because of hunger and starvation not necessarily because of Nigerian fire power. The war started as soon as the coup failed in 1966 but Igbos started fighting back only after May 29, 1967. By that time millions of Igbos had lost their lives, their properties around Nigeria, and their jobs in military and civil service of Nigeria.

THE FAILED ABURI PEACE CONFERENCE

The conference was held at a town called Aburi. In that conference, both leaders agreed on several issues some of which were:

(a) Stop the butchering of Igbo people;
(b) Call the Hausa soldiers back to barracks;
(c) Compensate the refugees;
(d) Return the civil servants under the federal civil service to their previous positions and
(e) Grant limited autonomy to the East, in other words for the Easterners to manage their affairs within the federation of Nigeria, thus, a "Confederate arrangement."

These and other agreements were never implemented. However, rumor had it that the British government advised Gowon against their implementations, especially on the confederacy issues. By disregarding these agreements, East was not given further alternative than to secede or to work out some defensive arrangements within Nigeria, as war was imminent. The war came and Biafra lost.

THE SECESSION

After the failed Aburi conference, demonstrations were held in various eastern provinces while people urged the military governor to take action or be removed. He was particularly asked to declare a republic, that is, an independent nation from Nigeria. It was obvious from the actions of all other ethnic groups that Igbo people are no more needed in Nigeria. On May 29, 1967, the chant "Nigeria is Dead, We are Biafrans" ran through the streets of major Eastern towns. On the midnight of that faithful day, the military governor of the East, Lt. Colonel Emeka Ojukwu, 33 announced the steps for secession and subsequently unfurled the banner of the *"Republic of Biafra."* Gowon however, denounced the secession as an act of rebellion, which he hoped to crush within 48 hours. He then ordered the mobilization of Nigeria forces and sent about two army battalions to the borders of the new nation. He also ordered the naval blockade of Biafran coasts to choke off the new nation's economy. In other words, he declared war on Biafra.

It finally occurred to the Igbo people that they should defend themselves. Biafrans started massive military draft unknown previously. Every young man or women showed up for the draft. The wake up call had been *"He who*

is surrounded by enemies must always be on guard, Biafrans do not sleep"
and people believed that they shall die but for a just cause. Literally, the people did not sleep for the next 35 months. Although armed with only local
weapons and ammunitions, the war, which Gowon declared on the people,
lasted for three years. The war was sustained on the fear of continued genocide, which had already occurred without a declared war. The fighting spirit
was very high. However, diplomatic successes and the world's sympathy
were counted on to win the war. Unfortunately, British were on the side of
Nigeria and convinced her allies to go along with them. Malnutrition and outright starvation killed more people in Biafra than the firepower of the vandals
as the Nigerian army was called. Workers of some international relief agencies reported then that as many as three thousand children and elderly were
dying daily and the total death may have reached about four million at the end
of hostilities.

THE BIAFRAN ADMINISTRATION

Although, Biafra remained in the state of emergency until its demise in 1970,
the new nation was managed in the Igbo political philosophy. There was a
constituent assembly of elders as well as military high command necessitated
by the state of emergency. While the military high command managed the security efforts, the assembly was charged with some form of legislative functions. The assembly, was divided into commissions and the chairman of the
assembly, was Dr. Alvan Ikokwu. The list of the commissions are; 'Atrocities,
Rehabilitation, Development, Food Directorate, Housing. Each of these commissions was headed by commissioners. Other commissioners were appointed to take charge of labor, rural development, education, transport, communication, and health and home affairs. Major (Dr.) Albert Okonkwo was
appointed to head the republic of Benin, which was liberated as the immediate task, to secure the life of Igbo people West of Niger.

Many international communities recognized Biafra. However, the initial
recognition was by those countries that share common ancestry with Igbo
people. They are—Tanzania, April 13, 1968; Gabon, May 8, 1968; Ivory
Coast (Cote d'Ivoire), May 14, 1968; Zambia, May 20, 1968; Haiti, March
22, 1969 as well as others. Some of these countries shared same cultural heritage. Biafra maintained the previous 20 provinces of eastern Nigeria while
the constituent assembly appointed provincial administrators to oversee the
affairs of each province. The provinces of Biafra and their respective administrators includes:—Aba-Moses Onwuma; Abakaliki- Samuel Mgbada; An-
nang - Ekpo Bassey; Awka - Paul Mgbada; Calabar - E. B. Ndem; Degema -

S. N. Dikibo; Eket - S. J. Edoho; Enugu - Christian C. Onoh; Nsukka - Frank Onyeke; Ogoja - Frank Ugbut; Oji River - G. O. Odenigwe; Okigwe - S. O. Mbakwe; Onitsha - R. I. Iweka; Opobo - S. J. Cookey; Orlu - R. I. Uzoma; Owerri - D. Njiribeako; Port Harcourt - E. Eguma; Uyo - J. Udoh Affiah; Yenegoa - Frank Opigo.

The entity known as Biafra consisted of the nine states existing in the present day South Eastern states of Nigeria, including Abia (*Umuahia*), Akwa-Ibom (*Uyo*), Anambra (*Awka*), Bayelsa (*Yenegoa*), Cross River (*Calabar*), Ebonyi (*Abakaliki*), Enugu (*Enugu*), Imo (*Owerri*), and Rivers (*Port Harcourt*). Within these nine states there are about 30 tribes consisting of *Ada-ada, Agbaja*, and *Wawa* in Enugu state; *Bende, Ebonyi, Egbema, Ihiala, Ika, Izza, Nri, Oka, Onicha, Owerri, Ngwa* known as central Igbo. Others are *An-donni, Anang, Abanyom, Anyima, Akajuk, Adun, Boki, Ikwerre, Degema, Ig-bani, Ejagham, Eket, Ekoi, Efik, Etche, Ibibio, Ibeno, Izon, Ikom, Iyala, Kana, Mbembe, Mbube, Nkum, Ogoni, Okobo, Oron, Kwa, Ukale*, and *Uyanga* etc.

LOSS OF BIAFRA AND CONSEQUENCES

By early 1970, Nigerian troops and some mercenaries fighting on their side encircled Biafra while occupying major cities. The Biafran capital was moved to Umuahia while Orlu was one other province free of Nigeria vandals. About eight million people were killed, while more than 6 million homes in various villages were destroyed. The leader of Biafra, General Odumegwu Ojukwu went into exile in Ivory Coast while his military assistant, General Philip Effiong surrendered to the vandals on 12 January 1970. It should be recalled that in the first republic, the Lagos Military junta had labored to separate the people of Rivers and Delta from Eastern region. While the war was raging, Gowon divided Nigeria into 12 states including the territories of Biafra. All the tribes within the central Igbo land were clumped together as 'East Central State' while the Delta region was divided into Rivers and Cross River States. At Lagos and Ibadan axis, Gowon sought out some young men, especially from the Universities, who were trapped by the war, who came originally from these Rivers and Cross River State. They were convinced that such separation from Igbo central would ensure the prosperity of their people after the war. Additionally, the entire Igbo wealth in their domain was to be confiscated with the aid of Nigeria army and handed over to them. Young people like Isaac Boro, Tam David West, and Kenneth Saro Wiwa etc., jumped to the bandwagon and took up arms against their own people. Fortunately for them, the war was lost mainly due to the sabotage of their cohort. These three renegade leaders were finally eliminated by the same Nigeria that propped them up.

The initial actions of these people were to advise their people on the change of people's and town names especially those that sounded Igbo. Those who bore names like Nwachukwu, changed to Wachuku, Nwali became Wali etc. Town's names were also changed such as Umuokoroshi to Rumukorosi, or Umuogba to Rumuogba etc. Fifteen years after the physical hostilities, they held tight to those names and prevented the people of the central to return to their homes in Port Harcourt and Calabar. Ironically, all Igbo properties in the Northern Nigeria were promptly returned to the owners immediately after the war. In fact, some of their friends collected rents on some properties during the war and these monies were given to such property owners, as soon as they were able to come back.

In 1982, Emeka Ojukwu was pardoned and he came back from exile amidst a tumultuous welcome by his people. He subsequently went to the supreme court of Nigeria in an attempt to reclaim his property at Queens Drive in Lagos, which was hitherto declared, abandoned property, like other Igbo properties in various parts of East and Western Nigeria. He won the battle, which opened a floodgate of litigation, leading to the reclamation of several thousands of houses owned by the Igbo people in Rivers, Southeast and Western Nigeria, which were previously described as abandoned property. Unfortunately, several houses had been badly damaged and abused by those who inherited them after the war. For all those number of years, Port Harcourt, a once beautiful garden city became an eye-sour. The harbor became clogged, while the Nigerian military that promised them prosperity did nothing to improve these facilities until the true owners of Port Harcourt came back.

IGBO MARGINALIZATION IN NIGERIAN STATE

During that war, Chief Awolowo, the father of political tribalism, who denied the great Zik the opportunity to form the government of Western region in 1954, became the highest-ranking civilian in Gowon's cabinet. He declared that hunger and starvation were legitimate weapons of war. He made Gowon to use such weapon against Igbo children viciously. In addition, Awolowo used his Yoruba brothers to replace the highly skilled Igbo technocrats in the Nigeria government. This was the principal reason why he supported abrogation of the Aburi agreement.

When the hostilities ended, the military and civil service positions held by Igbo people prior to the civil war were not returned to the Igbos. Chief Obafemi Awolowo, the Federal Commissioner for Finance, decreed that any Biafran, who so much deposited any amount in any Nigerian bank, would be entitled to twenty pounds only irrespective of how much money each depositor had in such banks before the civil war. He subsequently banned trade in some commodities such as stockfish and second hand clothing where Igbo people excelled. To finally seal the economic faith of Igbo people, he advised on a legislation to nationalize all foreign holdings in the Nigerian economy and stock market (indigenization Decree), when the average cash owned by most Igbo people was equivalent to US $40.

Up until 1990s, several years after the war, the Igbo people were still being discriminated against in appointments and promotions in public and military services. In fact, it became so irritating that in July of 1998, the Ohaneze Ndigbo, pan-Igbo umbrella organization of Igbo unions criticized severely the appointments made by the head of state of Nigeria, General Abdulsalami Abubakar, into the vacant positions in the armed forces. They warned that if those appointments were not reversed, it would become clear that the Marginalization of the Igbos was and still is the deliberate policies of the Nigerian people, military or civilians. They noticed that it was inconsistent with the posture of reconciliation, which that administration was presenting.

Today, groups of young Igbo people in Nigeria and abroad have continued the fight for freedom in the name of MASSOB (*Movement for the Actualization of the Sovereign State of Biafra*). Several of its leaders are currently languishing in various jails in Nigeria. The incarcerations generally did very little to dampen the quest for a new Igbo nation. There is a general disenchantment that pervades the thinking of most Igbo people, even in Diaspora. Despite that the wealth of the nation is based on single product oil, which is produced in several parts of Igbo land, up till the year 2007, there is no Federal government of Nigerian presence in Biafra Land.

Whereas most roads in other geopolitical zones are awarded to reputable and competent construction companies like Julius Berger, those in Biafra Land are awarded to less known and incompetent companies. And even at that, the roads are never completed but the contract money is always paid to those less competent companies in full. Simply put, the current Biafran roads are '*death-traps.*' The fact that the Biafra-Nigerian civil war ended 37 years ago is like a fairy tale to most Igbo people. The policemen and soldiers still act as if they are an occupying force in an enemy territory.

WAGES OF SABOTAGE AND RIVERRINE IGBOS

Ironically, although the deprivations and denials against Igbo people were astronomic, those who collaborated with the vandals to vanquish Biafra did not fair better. They seemed to have paid greater price for peace as much as the rest suffered in the war. At the end of it all, what the Riverrine Igbos who denied their brothers at the heat of the war did, came back to haunt them. Several years after the civil war the facilities in those two states remained in state of disrepair as much as those in the hinter land. However, because much of Nigeria crude came from these areas, their environment became highly polluted with crude oil spills. No resources were allocated to clean the environment or ameliorate the general poverty of the people. With time, the promise of Igbo property became hoarse and what ever they were able to inherit before returning them to the owners were not enough to upgrade their level of life. Igbo people came back from various refugee camps within and outside Biafra, and slowly but steadily rebuilt Port Harcourt, which was regarded as their garden city. They eventually prospered beyond the imaginations of all other Nigerians.

On the human angle, Isaac Boro did not live to share in the inheritance of Igbo properties. He died while fighting Biafra and killing his own people in Bonny sector of the war. In fact the blood of his people was avenged. Ken Saro Wiwa got the rope in the late 1980s from general Abacha for killing or masterminding the killing of 12 of his clan chiefs. Tam David West was jailed several times because of his demand for fair treatment of his people and the fulfillment of the military promise of better life to his people. The oil money sourced from these areas went mostly into the pockets of northern military officers and their cohorts. Few amounts that were used for public services went to the Petroleum Trust Fund, which concentrated in reconstruction of northern roads and social services. Meanwhile, there are no passable and paved roads in the whole of eastern Nigeria, including roads in those areas that helped the Lagos junta to destroy Biafra.

SYMBOLS OF BIAFRA

The National Anthem of Biafra:

Land of rising sun we love and cherish,
Beloved homeland of our brave heroes,
We must defend our lives or we shall perish
We shall protect our hearts from all our foes
But if the price is death for all we hold dear
Then let us die without a shred of fear.
Hail to Biafra, consecrated nation
Oh father land, this be our solemn pledge
The waving standard, which emboldens the free
Shall always be our flag of liberty.
We shall emerge triumphant from this ordeal
And although the crucible unscathed we'll pass

When we are poised the wounds of battle to heal
We shall remember those who died in mass
And then shall our trumpet peal the glorious song
Of victory we scored o'er might and wrong.
Oh God protect us from the hidden pitfall
Guide all our movements' lets we go astray
Give us the strength to head the humanistic call
'To give and not count the cost each day'
Bless those who rule to serve with resoluteness
To make this clime a land of righteousness

The national flag of Biafra contains the colors of Red, Black and Green stacked accordingly with a yellow star at the black middle strip. Rising sun was not only the symbol of Biafran struggle but also the symbol for East. It represented both the ancestral origin and the location of the Promised Land with respect to Nigerian land mass. The rising sun was worn by every soldier that fought for the empire of Nubia during which Egypt was incorporated under the general of people Army, Oku-Paleke (Piankhy). In the like manner, the Biafra soldiers proudly displayed the rising sun on the right shoulders of their army uniform during the Biafra-Nigerian conflict of 1967–1970.

The rising sun also showed some spikes that represented the provinces of Biafra. The Biafran Coat of Arm (BCA) shown in the Biafran currency was also produced from historical association with the greater Nubia. Similar Coat of Arm was displayed in the front gate of the ancient city of Meroe, which was the capital, or the administrative headquarters of Unubi-Igbo (Nubia). . The spikes on the rising sun are used to indicate some of its provinces.

Biafran Money

Although Biafra was lost in physical terms, psychologically it exists in mind and sole of true Igbo persons. The Biafran currency is still in circulation in parts of some West African countries, and by one account, in a community in New York also. And, it is not just a souvenir: it is legal tender in places like Ivory Coast and Ghana. Where it can be exchanged, one Biafran pound is worth 280 Naira, Nigerian Money.

It goes to prove the point that Biafra is really here to stay. The Spirit of Biafra is indomitable and indestructible. Countless numbers of Igbos in Diaspora have continued with the non-violent movement to actualize Biafra and reclaim her sovereignty and independence from Nigeria. Biafra bank notes[1] are in the denominations of 1, 5, 10 and 20. They seem to be an intriguing set of notes and will provide a collector with a complete set of a 'country' for an affordable price. Many collectors will be familiar with the events of the Nigerian civil war, and equally there will be many younger collectors who have little or no memory of the events. The information in this book should be of interest to both old and young collectors, and will hopefully illuminate an important piece of African history—as well as the history of the Biafran struggles. The palm tree in the middle of the bank note symbolizes the original economic strength of Igbo people. The tree, as explained in chapter 5 has all round utility. Crude oil revenue has, in recent time relegated its importance to the background but it continues to play a big role in the economy of the people. Igbo people like the legendry palm tree can and will do all things through Chineke that strengthen them.

The front piece of the Note contains the "Biafran Coat of Arm." When the Nigerian Military constructed the war Museum at Umuahia, they sort after the Coat of Arm to be part and parcel of the institution. In order to display it along with other war relics, including Igbo made artilleries, armored cars and shore batteries, Nigerian government spend reasonable sum of money and even pardoned General Ojukwu. They reasoned that with such material at large, it will be difficult to seal the faith of the struggle. If indeed the coat of arms comes into their possession, the people will be discouraged to put up another resistance since the symbol of their power was under the control of Nigeria, they reasoned. The Biafran Ideology, "Ahiara Declaration", however is currently in circulation in Nigeria and around the world.

THE CHRONICLE OF IGBO MASSACRE

The immediate cause of the Biafran-Nigerian conflict in the 1960s after the failed Major Nzeogwu's coup was the massacre of Igbo people in all parts of Nigeria especially in Northern Nigeria. However, Igbo people had periodically suffered several of such massacres for even inconsequential reasons in the past. In 1945 for instance, rail road workers and coal miners at Enugu called for general strike. The colonial administration refused to negotiate with the striking workers. Since much of the supplies needed in the Northern part of Nigeria came from the sea and being transported by rail, scarcity of goods including food items resulted in the North. The District Officer representing the colonial administration blamed the Igbos. Igbo people were then killed and maimed at the cosmopolitan city of Jos.

In 1953, a member of Action Group (a Yoruba political organization) tabled a motion for Nigerian Independence for 1956. The Northern Leaders indicated that they were not ready and subsequently tabled a counter motion that shall effectively delay the de-colonization of the people. They instead prefer a language that abrogated the specific date of 1956 but included "as soon as possible." When the counter motion failed, they blamed Igbo members of NCNC, and then instigated a riot in the North that took several lives of innocent Igbos among them. The mayhem was said to have lasted from May 16 to 19 of that year. When five Majors in the Nigerian Army took law into their hand to change government because of the perceived corruption tendency of the civilian administration, the coup was only partially successful. The higher ranking officers, took charge, imprisoned the Majors and decreed a unitary government. The people of Northern Nigeria objected. The Military boys of Northern origin then planned a systematic execution of Igbo people in the military. These attacks originated in a military garrison in Zaria. Several days later, it spread like a wild fire and went through other Northern cities where even non-military Igbo people were systematically killed.

When General JTU Ironsi was assassinated in Ibadan along with his host on May 29, 1966 Igbo people again became a target of destruction from the hand of both the Yoruba and Hausa/Fulani soldiers and civilians. The North, it seemed was retaliating the killing of Sarduana of Sokoto as well as the Prime Minister, Tafawa Balewa but the Yoruba interest was to steal and vandalize the properties of Igbo people in Lagos and Ibadan. Also, the Yoruba people were interested in removing all vestiges of Igbo hold on the civil service system of Nigeria. About 10,000 Igbo people were reportedly killed within Lagos and Ibadan axis alone. At this time, it seemed that law and order had finally broken down and up until September and November of 1966; this has in fact turned into "Genocide." The killing of Igbos expanded to every nook and cranny of Nigeria, and perhaps except the Eastern region not less than a million people lost their lives. Igbo properties estimated to worth about one billion Pounds were sieved, vandalized and destroyed. Physical structures were taken and military junta in Lagos and Kaduna supported these systematic stealing of properties, which they termed "abandoned properties." Churches were burned down, Igbo schools were destroyed and Igbo people found in the process, men women and children were not spared. Their bodies were buried in mass graves while some are gathered and burnt alive in places such as Kano and Katsina. Again, about a million Igbos did not make it to the East and no person accounted for them even until today.

Awolowo, the only civilian member of the Nigerian supreme military council advised Colonel Gowon to effectively blockade Biafra and prevent relief supplies to the people. He told BBC news report that hunger and starvation was a legitimate instrument of warfare and that they would fully exploit it. International organizations and NGO's were prohibited from sending food and medicine to Biafran children. This attempt at Igbo extermination has since become the standard by which human cruelty and suffering are measured. In fact Awolowo and others should have faced war crime tribunals if in fact there was an International Justice. Killing of Igbo people has continued in one form to another and for one reason to another. In February 2006, Muslims in Northern Nigeria city of Maiduguri protesting caricatures of Mohammed published in Denmark, attacked Igbo people and burned their churches. This violence left dozens dead and injured. In quite a rare happenstance, Igbo people retaliated by killing Muslims and burning mosques at Onitsha and Aba.

RENEWED QUEST FOR ACTUALIZATION OF BIAFRA

Igbo agitations for independence arose out of frustration brought about by first, the genocide directed against the people in the 1960's and secondly, the marginalization practices of both military and civilian governments of Nigeria after the war. They left Nigeria as refugees and returned to Nigeria as refugees. Property owners in most parts of Nigeria were denied access to them. Lt. Colonel Yakubu Gowon and his Yoruba supporters said, at the heat of war propaganda, that they were fighting to keep Nigeria one. However after the war, Igbo people discovered that Nigeria fought Biafra to keep the crude oil one and that indeed they have no need for those whose land contained the oil wells. Vivid example is the turn of events in the Delta areas of Nigeria where oil prospectors have completely polluted the waters and agricultural lands of the people without an adequate compensation.

Without adequate respite, Igbo people around the world formed an organization with the aim of securing the resurgence of the defunct Biafran state. The organization is named "Movement for the Actualization of the Sovereign State of Biafra (MASSOB)" while its sphere of operation is within the territorial Nigeria. The Biafran flag is hoisted over and flies throughout the enclave formerly known as Biafra. This is said to be a reminder that although there was a defeat, victory would soon be achieved.

MASSOB is fashioned as a non-violent civil right movement. Currently, it has no armed group and uses persuasions and education to mobilize its members. It is led by Mr. Ralph Uwazuruike and its headquarters is at Okwe in Okigwe area of Imo State. Since its inception, MASSOB has had many conflicts with Nigerian Police and army. In 2006, they accused the leader of this movement of treason, felony and other offenses. The irrational reaction of Nigerian government to this peaceful movement has helped to keep the organization alive and in fact, the movement activities have been in the news almost on daily basis. Its members around the world have continued to condemn the overreaction of the government of Nigeria. They have, in many instances deplored the government's action of sending the army and police to kill and maim people because they are on the peaceful march which is guaranteed in the so called 1999 constitution of Nigeria.

In the year 2000, a United Nation Human Right Organization[2] reported that several people were injured at a weekend rally in Okigwe after Nigerian government deployed soldiers to curb the activities of secessionist movement (MASSOB). The movement was said to be enforcing the control price of gasoline commodity in the city. In that incident, a privately owned newspaper, "This Day" reported that two people were killed by the soldiers. In March 2001, the movement wondering why transportation fuel produced in Biafra should be more expensive here than anywhere else in Nigeria, warned that the organization would start the seizure of loaded fuel tankers moving from any part of Biafra to the north or west with effect from April 1. The legal adviser to the movement explained that the measure would only be suspended when the Federal government of Nigeria and NNPC redress the existing imbalances and inequity inherent in the distribution of petroleum products in the country. In July 2006 the center for World Indigenous studies reported that Igbos was being killed at Onitsha. That the government had ordered shoot-to-kill policy directed to members of MASSOB. The killing and maiming of Igbos would continue since oil continues to be the only export good in Nigeria. The intention is to scare them and ensure that other parts of Nigeria continue to exploit the land and resources of Igbo people.

NOTES

1. The Bank Notes, UN agencies, donors, human rights organizations, political parties, regional institutions, churches, academia, businesses and the media around the world.

2. United Nation Sub Commission who undertake studies and recommend the prevention of discrimination of any kind relating to human rights and fundamental freedom.

The Chronicle of Igbo People

THE SUMMARY

The Main Idea

"Adventures of Ojemba" is a story of Igbo people. It has not chosen to dwell on any particular issue or episode affecting Igbo people. It rather gave a general overview of 'Who they are; What they do, their traditions and culture that sets them apart from their neighbors, as well as some problems they had faced in recent times.' The specific motivation for writing this book was the realization that certain basic questions that could be asked about Igbo people or people of any culture for that matter, were after all, not so basic. In specifics, questions like *"Who are the Igbo People?"* does not really provide a simple explanation or an answer. However, this book tried to provide some probable answers by developing a theory along the part of Igbo people being part of the black Jews, which had been a common view of most historians. They were therefore the group that developed empires of Aksum, Cush, Nubia and Sheba etc., which existed in the horn of Africa in ancient times.

Why Saba Theory May be a Possibility

Based on cultural similarities and activities likely of Igbo traditions in those ancient kingdoms, and because the tomb of the Queen of Sheba was finally found in Igbo land, this book developed a theory of the people being the descendants of Adwa, the queen of Sheba. The great queen on her part was also the descendant of Abraham through Kedema the last child of Ishmael. These people were adventurers while they developed considerable knowledge and skills relevant for creating empires and kingdoms without them being absorbed. They produced several kings and emperors including Pharaohs of

101

Egypt such as Ptolemy and Cleopatra whose African name was Iputu. They had moved to central and then to West Africa because these various kingdoms declined and because they remained strangers in such lands amongst indigenous people whom they had ruled. This book also tried to imply that some of such movements were really ordained so that they could find their Promised Land. On arriving to the area, east of River Niger and North of Atlantic Ocean, where they inhabited for about 500 years without external aggression, they proclaimed that they had reached the Promised Land. Every literature on the origin of Igbo people is in general agreement that Igbo traditions and culture were similar to that of the Hebrews in the Middle East. However, two prolific Igbo writers, Professor Adiele Afigbo and Dr. Elizabeth Isichie claimed that there is core Igbo nation (Okigwe, Owerri and Orlu) that perhaps did not come from anywhere. That theory however, defies the logic behind evolution or that of creation since archeologists have determined that the earliest man that evolved on earth was probably in the Northeast of Africa. God also created the first human in a place the bible described as "Garden of Eden". Since that core Igbo nation may not be the said Garden of Eden, the core nation theory does not stand. Igbo people therefore originated from the center of evolution as described by archeologist.

The Religious Philosophy of the People

The traditional religion of the people was unique while appeared strange to the people surrounding them. They believed that religious faith and philosophical understanding are complementary. However, in the ancient times, while still in the horn of Africa, they accepted the "Coptic Christianity," although without much understanding. They believed in one Supreme Being, which they called Chineke, God of creation. They combined ethical and supernatural beliefs into a spiritualistic view of life basing such beliefs on the fact that souls are prisoners of the body. Souls are freed at death, and reincarnated in a higher or lower form of life, depending on the degree of virtues achieved.

The Development of the Promised Land

This book highlighted their occupational successes and their participation in the founding of modern day Nigeria. The colonialism, although destroyed some important elements of their culture, provided avenues for urbanization, modernization and new ways of life. Aba and Onitsha, two most important commercial cities in Africa were created out of their interaction with Europeans. They also lost a lot of their people to the New World. However, the greatness of the United States of America was partly as a result of the people working the farms of the New World. Before the Europeans came to the homeland of Igbo people, the people maintained their culture, used such culture to maintain law and order in their clans and villages. They constructed their mud brick houses in the fashion of the ancient Egyptian culture, hunted, fished and farmed. They made pottery at Okigwe and Umunze, they built firearms at Nkwere, they wove cotton garments at Akwette, and they mined salt at Ishiagu and Uburu etc. They operated a simple but effective government system where elders held sway, which was the envy of the world of the ancient times. There were no separation between government and religion while the two functioned to maintain some traditional institutions.

The breeds of livestock and varieties of crops they farmed in their homeland were completely different from the ones produced by their neighbors. These unique agricultural commodities were rather similar to those farmed or produced in East African sub region, specifically, in the southern Sudan, Kenya, Uganda, Tanzania etc. Igbo people therefore must have lived in the horn of Africa but may have originated from the Asia Minor because the empire known in the ancient time as Sheba is currently replaced by Yemen. However, power struggles between their leaders and the original inhabitants of these areas as well as political and environmental instability may have precipitated some of the wars, defeats, and general movements to hinterlands of African continent.

Their Fate in Modern Day Nigeria

Even in their homeland, the founding of Nigeria and their subsequent attempt to govern the place created events that led to the Biafran wars of 1965–1970. The Biafra war was lost and Igbo people have not yet recorded the ripple effect of that loss. For those brief periods in human history, the Nigerian Nation, the handiwork of British Empire and Igbo people, was nearly destroyed. Although it survived the trauma, it has remained unstable since the empire creators; thus the Igbo people who helped create Nigeria are still being marginalized and generally mistreated.

Scarcity of Information on Igbo History

Most books on the history of West Africa may briefly mention Igbo people but it is quite rare to find one that can give details or to discuss fully the people's culture, even when such authors are of Igbo origin. There are three main reasons why it was so. One reason may perhaps be that the Igbo homeland was not considered part of West Africa until the British conquest of the Niger River basins. All historical accounts of the sub region predated the amalgamation of several kingdoms that made up the present day Nigeria. The area of Igbo homeland may have been part of Central Africa along with Southern Cameroon.

Secondly, because Igbo people have a unique distinct culture, which is different from other West African people, historians felt that the people may have been strangers and were not part of the sub region. Thirdly, historians have the tendency of analyzing the leadership of kingdoms including command structures of the army both of which were not existing in Igbo land but existed in Ghana, Mali, Yoruba, Benin, Hausa and Songhay empires of West Africa. As there was no feudal king or any kind of centralized government system and no standing army of occupation commanded by an Igbo general, historians assumed that there were no historical events in Igbo land worth noting.

Although this book is modeled as an entertainment piece, it would be a supplementary text for African Studies around the world. It would also be important to the students of literature, secular or ecclesiastical historians as well as philosophy. It contains view points that may not have been covered by the writings of notable Igbo historians such as Professor Adiele Afigbo or Dr. Elizabeth Isichie. These distinguished individuals have made a lot of contribution in the process of promoting Igbo culture; however their writings are highly technical and may not be quite easily absorbed by ordinary readers.

Written Records of Igbo Culture

Very few authors however ventured into the area of disclosing Igbo culture to the world comprehensively. These various writers suggested various origins due to the cultural manifestations. Igbo culture and traditions before the coming of the Europeans are similar to the traditions of the ancient Hebrews. Some therefore suggested that they might have been black Jews who have migrated from the horn of Africa into their present location. One prominent literature was the "History of Igbo People" written by Dr. Elizabeth Isichie. She gave a lot of factual information about the people while in part supporting this popular theory and in other angle, discussed the existence of core Igbo nation with claims that they originated from the area. The contention of the present book is that Igbo people came from Saba province, which was a part of Ethiopia before it grew into a recognizable empire under Ada Akeze popularly known as the 'Queen of Sheba.' She was also a descendant of the Biblical Ishmael, the first son of Abraham. Biblical account indicates that Ishmael and his mother were expelled from the land of Canaan when he was a boy. They settled at Havilar Shur near Egypt. Wars, adventures and expeditions may have prompted their movement into the continental Africa and to the present location since Sheba was situated at the present day Yemen. They crossed into Ethiopia ruling the empire for a while before creating even a more viable empire called Nubia.

Where Igbo people inhabit today is the forest region of West Africa which is assumed to be their promised land and to locate the Promised Land, they passed through the Congo basins, the Cameroon Mountains, the plateau areas of the Central West African Savanna, then Ekoi/Ogoja axis, before arriving between 500 BC and AD 200. They were associated with the iron technology of the famous Nok culture. Archeologists at the present day Jos/Lafia axis had found the relics of such civilization. This book tried to proffer suggestions of why they were in each location at one time or the other. The book also tried to unravel the issues of the Igbo and Jewish cultural similarities which has always been used as a yard stick for suggesting that Igbos are the black Jews.

This book therefore is a supplement to Mrs. Isichie's history text. What this book has contributed mainly is the accounts of the travails of Igbo people during and after independence of Nigeria. Such travail includes Biafran wars of 1967–1970. Although, those aspects of Igbo history have had a lot of coverage both in the media and in other literary world, we feel that a lot of information was still being deliberately sidetracked especially on the issues of *Reconciliation, Reconstruction, and Marginalization.* Marginalization issue has caused not only mass migration of Igbo people to all parts of the world but it has cost Nigeria in terms of brain drain. The mass movement out of Igbo land therefore put significant strain on the culture of the people. Some elements of Igbo culture are now going extinct. This book tried to record such cultures as *reincarnation, Ogbanje, Ajohia*, etc., as well as document significant number of idioms and proverbs which was said to be the butter of the bread of Igbo spoken/language culture.

Why the Book Was Written

Many non-Africans think of Africa as a continental village where people ought to be their brother's keepers. Such people often wonder why there should be wars especially within a national boundary. However, the only thing common to Hutus and Tutsi's living in one country is the color black and perhaps the artificial national territory created by white man during their scramble for Africa. It goes for different people occupying the present day Nigeria. To those who created Nigeria out of about five kingdoms that existed before 1900 in the Niger Delta region, there were no differences among the people. Having conflicts in Nigeria seemed to them to be family's feud because they lack the basic understanding of the culture of the people and their differences. To the British particularly, Nigeria is community where every people within ought to understand each other, dance and sing the same way and even eat the same type of dish.

However, more than four hundred ethnic groups exist in Africa generally. Therefore more than four hundred ways of life of the people exist. People may have migrated to the area from different corners of Africa and they came with their unique traditions and culture, which non-Africans are not aware of. For centuries, although with some adulterations, different people have maintained their differences within such artificial national boundaries. This book is written so that many non-Africans and indeed Africans born in Diaspora can appreciate such diversities of culture that exist in the continent.

Igbo Diaspora Population and Igbo Culture

Emeka may not have the opportunity to read some exotic Igbo literatures such as "*Ije Odumodu, Ala Bingo, Omenuko etc.*," He may not have been told the folk tales *of "The Gong and Eagle Tails; or Adventures of Tortoise, Hare and Spider.*" They made the Igbo oral literature the world class. He may never been given the opportunity to study the language "*Ibo*" which is suppose to be his vernacular. These deprivations were because, although born of Igbo parents, Emeka was raised in Northern Nigeria, in a cosmopolitan city of Makurdi where the dominant culture is '*Tiv.*'

Few times Emeka visited his grand fathers in Igbo homeland; he was always confused listening to them because they interjected all their conversations with either proverbs or idioms. To his grandfathers, the confusion was mainly because he was not properly educated. They expected a well-educated Igbo person to interpret and act upon simple proverbs and idioms used in every day conversation in Igbo families. Emeka's dilemma is not unique to him. The reference is to the millions of Igbo kids born and bred in Diaspora. Considering these handicaps, a sudden realization came to me that they probably would never be able to unravel the mysteries of their own origin. These mysteries may be unraveled by the accounts contained in this book. The book may motivate the children to start the exploration of the meaning of their people's existence.

Appendix

SHORT BIOGRAPHY OF PEOPLE THAT
SHAPED IGBO HISTORY

ABRAHAM: He was the father of both Isaac and Ishmael, to whom all the Jews claim descendants.

ACHEBE, CHINUA: He has been very prolific in writing about Igbo Culture and a professor of African literature. He was born in Ogidi in the present day Anambra State. He has won many awards.

ADWA (ADA): This is the first name of the famous queen of ancient empire of Saba whom Igbo claim descendants. It is also a name of a city in Ethiopia founded by Menelik II, the son of the great queen.

AKAZA (AKAEZE): This was the grand child of Kedema and an Ethiopian prince and the father of Adwa, the Queen of Saba.

ASIKA, UKPABI: One time administrator of a defunct East Central State created in the heat of Biafran War. He married a Chinyere Ejiogu, the daughter of a prominent public officer in colonial administration from Egbu near Owerri

AZIKIWE, NNAMDI: Zik was the first premier of Eastern Region of Nigeria, the first African governor general of Nigeria and the first president of the Federal Republic of Nigeria. He held an Igbo traditional title of Owelle of Onitsha and was fondly called Zik of Africa in recognition of his role in creation of the "Organization of African Unity." He was born in 1904 in Zungeru near Minna in modern day Niger State by Igbo parents. He was the leader of NCNC as well as NPP political organizations. He was a journalist and Chancellor of the University of Lagos from 1972–1975.

CLEOPATRA: Queen Cleopatra as she was known was born Iputu by the second wife of a Nubian emperor called Piankhy (Oku-Paleke). She usurped the position of Pharaoh after she assassinated Ptolemy XIII also the child of the emperor of greater Nubia. She was a mistress of Roman emperor called Caesar from where she acquired the name Cleopatra. She later married Mark Anthony when Caesar was assassinated in 44 BC. She committed suicide by snakebite after a defeat in a war with Romans in Alexandria.

EKWUEME, ALEXANDER (Dr.): He is a national leader and an architect by profession. He was born at Oko, Anambra State where he built a college of Education, a polytechnic, and a number of social structures designed to better the life of his people. He became the first executive vice president of the Federal Republic of Nigeria from 1979–1983. His party "National Party of Nigeria (NPN)" won again for another four years but soon after the inauguration, a gang of military hoodlums, led by former petroleum minister Mohammed Buhari, overthrew their government. However, several years after he suffered some incarceration in the hands of Buhari and Idiagbon, he led a group of 34 eminent Nigeria to oppose military regimes. When Abacha died in 1998, he transformed that group of 34 into a formidable political party that won the national election in 1999.

ENWEREM, EVANS: The "mature" was a native of Atta in Imo State of Nigeria. He served as civilian governor of Imo State. In 1998, he was elected the senator from Owerri zone, and he subsequently became the senate president. The position he lost in late 1999 for some charges of fraud.

EMECHETA, BUCHI: This author of various novels is a native of Ikai Igbo, in Delta state. She studied sociology in London England. Her most important novel, "Destination Biafra" described the ordeal of Igbo people during that struggle.

ENWONWU, BEN: Ben was famous for sculpture artistry. He won several awards for his contributions in world art.

EZEIFE, CHUKWUEMEKA: He was the first civilian governor of smaller Anambra state, when Enugu and Abakaliki were removed from the Anambra. His state capital was Awka.

EKWIANO, OLAUDA: An Igbo boy from Onicha Ugbo in the old Benin Kingdom sold into slavery to the New World. After his freedom, he wrote his autobiography with a pseudonym of Gustavus Vassa in 1800's in England. He was probably the first to create Ibo alphabets.

HAGAR: Mother of Ishmael, second wife of Biblical Abraham. In her distress, the angel of the lord appeared to her in Beersheba. She took her son back to Egypt where she found a wife for him among her kin's.

IBIAM, AKANU: The first and only Eastern Regional Governor from 1958 to 1966. He was later crowned the traditional King of Unwana in Afikpo local government. Several institutions were named after him including a Polytechnic at Unwana.

IFEAJUNA: He was a major in the Nigerian Army before the Civil war of Biafra. He later fought on the side of Biafra and was the commander of the brigade that liberated Benin during the early days of Biafra. He was later accused of sabotage for abandoning his post after reaching Ore a major town in the Yoruba country.

IGBOKWE, CHRISTI: Mrs. Igbokwe performed as Akpino in a famous television sitcom called the Masquerade staring, Zeburudaya. She later became a musical legend and was popularly being referred to as, the first lady of Nigerian pop music. She won several musical awards.

IKE, CHUKWUEMEKA: A novelist and one time Registrar of the West African Examination Council in Lagos.

IKOKWU, ALVAN: Alvan was a foremost educationist and politician from Arochukwu. He was the chairman of Biafran constituent assembly of elders. As a commemoration of his contributions to creating Nigerian federation, his face was used to engrave one of the Nigerian currencies. Naming after him also immortalized him, an advanced teacher training college in Owerri, "Alvan Ikokwu College of Education."

IKOKWU, S. G.: The first son of Alvan, Samuel Grace Ikokwu was a socialist and belongs to parties that opposed his father's political association. In early 1980's he ran unsuccessfully as the vice presidential candidate of "People's Redemption Party" of Alhaji Aminu Kano.

IRONSI, AGUIYI: He was an army general and the only Africa to command a contingent of United Nation's Peace keeping force in Katanga between the years of 1959–1960. He crushed the first military coup carried out by some Majors in Nigerian Army. He later became the commander in Chief of Nigerian Armed Forces as well as the head of state of Nigeria in 1966. Rival Hausa soldiers in Ibadan assassinated him in July of 1966.

ISHMAEL: He was the first son of Abraham and Hagar. His name was translated to Nwachukwu in Ibo because of the circumstances before and after his birth. He fathered Kedema, (Ukeneme in Ibo) whom Igbo people claimed descendant.

ISICHIE, ELIZABETH: She was the author of many books dealing with Africa and a professor of history at the University of Nigeria, Nsukka. One of her publication was the "History of Igbo People."

KEDEMA (Ukeneme): He was the last child of Ishmael and the grand father of the queen of Sheba. He opened the settlement of Saba as a province of Ethiopia. He married an Ethiopian princess and helped made Maarib an important commercial city in ancient world.

MBAKWE, S. O.: Dee Sam was the only civilian executive governor of old Imo state. After him and couple of military governors, the state was split into Imo and Abia. He is an attorney of great repute and played significant role in fighting the "Abandon Property Issues." He was a member of the "Nigerian People's Party" (NPP) and an achiever. He was popularly known as the weeping governor because of the ferocity with which he pursued the concerns of his people.

MBANEFO, LOUIS: A political juggernaut, a distinguished lawyer, one time attorney general of Eastern Region and also served as justice of the federal high court.

MENELIK: Menelik was an emperor and subsequently, the ruling house of the ancient Ethiopian empire. The holder of Menelik II was the son of the queen of Sheba. The wise king of Israel, Solomon David, was said to be his biological father. The original Menelik was the grand father of the queen.

MUNONYE, JOHN: John was a novelist and a native of Akokwa in Ideato north of Imo State. Among his novels is "The only son."

NWACHUKWU: Ibo name meaning "Son of God." It was the Igbo people's translation of Ishmael, based on their system of naming people and places.

NWACHUKWU, IKE: He retired as a Nigerian army general. This army general served Nigeria in many capacities including as a military governor of Imo State during Buhari-Idiagbon regimes and as minister of Foreign affairs during Babangida regime (1985–1993). He commanded the first battalion based in Kano Nigeria and was credited to the foiling of Major David Okaa coup of 1991 against Babangida. Although, a native of Ovim in Isikwuato of Abia state, he was born and bred in Katsina royal house in Northern Nigeria.

NWANNA, PITA Author of "Omenuko," an Igbo story adapted from a life history of Igwegbe Odum, an uncle to K. O. Mbadiwe, a political leader and a nationalist. Pita Nwanna was a native of Aro-Ndizuogu in Ideato North of Imo State.

NWOBODO, JIM: The first executive and the only executive governor of old Anambra state before it was split into New Anambra and Enugu states. He was imprisoned by the Buhari-Idiagbon regime for political reasons (1984–1986). He later became the minister in charge of sports and culture in Abacha government. He ran unsuccessfully for the president of Nigeria in 1998. In 1999, he became one of the three Enugu State senators in the National assembly.

NWODO, OKWESILIEZE: A prominent surgeon turned politician became the governor of Enugu State after its creation in 1992. He was an executive member of People's Democratic Party created by Dr. Ekwueme and his associates after the death of General Abacha.

NWOSU, HUMPHREY: He was a political science professor at the University of Nigeria Nsukka. He served as the chairman of the National Electoral Commission that conducted the ill-fated election of June 12, 1993, which, was annulled by the military. Among his innovations in Nigerian politics that has endured till today, was the "option A4 voting pattern" as well as the open ballot system. All were designed to minimize rigging of elections.

NZEOGWU, CHUKWUMA: He became prominent in Nigeria after the "Exercise Damissa II," when he led five other majors in the Nigerian army to topple the government of Alhaji Abubakar Tafawa Balewa. The mismanagement occurred in the exercise when the politicians in AG and NCNC were spared in what could have been the bloodiest coup ever in Africa. He was a native of Okpanam near Asaba in the present day Delta state. He fought on the side of Biafra and mysteriously disappeared in the battle of Benin. His body was never found.

OGBALU, F. C.: Francis was an author and inventor of modern Ibo language. He arranged the language of Igbo people in grammatical sequence and invented names for several items that were recently introduced to the land through international exposures. He was a native of Onitsha in Anambra State.

OJIKE, MBONU: Mbonu was the first finance minister of Eastern regional government in the 1950's. He was a political activist and a nationalist to the core. He introduced and preached cultural preservation in view of foreign corruption of Igbo culture. He was a native of Aro-Ndizuogu in Ideato North of Imo State. He was immortalized with a hospital named after him.

OKAFO, DONALD: Don was one of the five majors that carried out the first military coup of 1966 in Nigeria. He was imprisoned after the failure of that coup, at Abeokuta, where Hausa soldiers abducted and killed him in cold blood.

OKONKWO, ALBERT: A medical doctor and an army major in the Nigerian army, who fought on the side of Biafra. He was Asaba indigene and was appointed the administrator of the Republic of Benin by the Biafran military high command.

OKU-OPALEKE (PIANKHY): He was the emperor of greater Nubia and father of two successive Pharaohs of Egypt (Ptolemy and Cleopatra). He conquered Egypt in 725 BC and established the 25th dynasty. His picture and that of other black Pharaohs survived in the Egyptian tombs.

HISTORICAL PLACES AND IMPORTANT TOWNS

Abia: This is a state in Igbo land containing Bende, Umuahia and Aba provinces. It is the home of the first indigenous brewery company called "Golden Guinea." It has a state owned University and two Federal research Institutes.

Ahiaragu: This is the first Igbo capital city in the present homeland before coal was found at Enugu Ngwo. The place is now the part of Plateau state of Nigeria. It is still famous for yam markets.

Aksum: An Empire derived from Ethiopia where King Ezana ruled. It was from the area that the people accepted Coptic Christianity and at the same time kept the Jewish ark of covenant, which is still in existence until today.

Alaba: This is a famous market existing in Lagos Nigeria created by Igbo traders for distributing household electronics.

Anambra: This a state in Igbo land named after a tributary of river Niger. It was carved out of old Anambra state now consisting of Awka and Onitsha provinces of Biafra.

Asaba: The last burial place of Queen of Sheba is the home of Ikai-Igbos west of River Niger in Nigeria. The name was probably derived from Saba, a former province of Ethiopia that grew into a kingdom. They maintained the name because they received the assignment of relocating the burial tomb of the queen of Sheba (Queen Adwa).

Awka: Former colonial capital of Central Igbo land is now the capital city of Anambra state of Nigeria. It is the Home of Nnamdi Azikiwe University after the first president of Nigeria who originated from there.

Biafra: An Igbo nation state that came into existence on May 29, 1967 in response to the genocide perpetrated against Igbo people in various locations in Nigeria. It ceased to exist after they were defeated in a three-year war against the Hausas and the Yoruba tribe.

Cameroon: A country in the central Africa; The southern Cameroon, which was part of Igbo land was ceded to French and German territory after the 1962 plebiscite.

Darfur: This is an ancient city in the Nubian empire and a trading outlet of Igbo ancestors. The Arabs are currently killing and maiming the Igbo relatives and citizens of southern Sudan.

Ebonyi: The latest state carved out of Abia State containing Ohaozara, Afikpo, and Abakaliki provinces. The area is famous for the production of long grain varieties of rice and other dry season vegetables. It is also the place in Igbo land where cattle and local cows are kept.

Enugu-Ngwo: Coal was discovered in southern hill of Ngwo. The commercial and industrial consequence of the find created Enugu metropolis and the former capital of Eastern Nigeria and subsequently of Biafra.

Imo: A river and a tributary of River Nigeria used to name a state in Igbo land. The state is the home of Orlu, Owerri and Okigwe people of Igbo origin. It has the oldest advance teachers college (Alvan), college of technology and two Universities.

Ikwerre: Riverrine Igbo people near Port Harcourt.

Cush (Kush): This was an Igbo empire created by King Opaleke (Piankhy) out of the ruins of Aksum. It is synonymously called Nubia after the territory was enlarged to include present-day southern Egypt, Sudan and Ethiopia.

Meroe: This a city designated as the seat of government of Kush and an important center of iron technology and trade in the ancient times. It had rich iron deposits as well as neighboring forest to provide fuel. Large slag heaps from ancient time indicates that Igbo people used smelting iron. It is now part of southern Sudan.

Nubia (Unubi-Igbo): This is a name of one of the most powerful empires in the region of modern day Sudan, Egypt and Ethiopia ruled by Igbo ancestors. The history was obscured because the language was not translated until Igbo alphabets were created out of English language. However, archeological finds and remains provide evidence of an advanced culture and civilization.

Unubi: An Igbo province of modern day Anambra State of Nigeria named after Nubia. It is believed that the people were the direct descendants of the royal families and is related to the Ikai Igbos as first cousins.

SOME IGBO WORDS FOUND IN THE TEXT AND THEIR MEANING

Afo: The first day of Igbo 4-day week; stomach, or year;

Agbara: Spirit of the night

Agwu: spirit sanctuary

Aja: Sacrifices offered to God through the high priest of spirit

Ajaro: Symbol of decency required to be established before a title is conferred to Igbo person.

Aku-Ohibo: Coconut tree or products thereof.

Ala: Land, the spirit that controls the fertility of lands as well as the morality of Igbo people.

Amuma: Lightening or the spirit of thunder and lightning.

Chi: Personal Spirit or guiding spirit

Chineke: God of creation or another name for Chukwu

Chukwu: Almighty God and the Lord of all spirits.

Dibia: Traditional doctors, soothsayers and/or herbalists.

Egusi: A crop and a member of melon family. Igbo people use the seeds to prepare vegetable soup.

Eke Iputu: The royal python

Eke" Python, Creation or the third day of Igbo 4-day market

Ekpe: One of the titles available for taking in Igbo land.

Ichi: The highest level of Ozo title in many Igbo communities.

Igwe: Heaven; Heavenly bodies or the title of the king of Orlu province or of Umunne Oha in Owerre division or province.

Ihejioku: The spirit that guided Igbo ancestors to the yam crop in the wilderness.

Ikeji: The first feast celebrated before the New Year by the Aro-Igbo people. It is also a method of yam preservation.

Iko: Drinking cup, or adultery.

Ikpo: Domestic bowl/dish made out of wood carving mainly from iroko tree.

Ikwe: Larger version of Ikpo or mortar for pounding/grinding food in Igbo.

Ilu: Proverbs, Idioms or parables

Iyi-Uwa: The symbol and/or power of reincarnation

Izu: Igbo week consisting of Afo, Nkwo, Eke and Orie,

Ji: Yam: The king of crops farmed in Igbo land.

Kitikpa: The spirit of smallpox, chicken pox and leprosy.

Mbekwu: Tortoise, prominent character in Igbo folktale.

Mbiarambia: Strangers, visitors, surjonars

Mkpaa-ji: A row of yam in yam barn, or the hunt for yam leftovers after the cropping season.

Mmanwu: Returning souls or spirits of ancestors in form of masquerades.

Ngwo: Raffia palm, or fresh wine from the tree

Nnu: One unit of counting in Igbo grammar, the word specifically represents 400.

Nwamba: Another prominent Igbo folktale character, pussycat.

Obi: The central family building; a family conference center and the dwelling of the family head; descendants of the octogenarian, a name of a person and/or the title of the king of Onitsha.

Of eke: Also honor, drunk, foolish individual

Ofo: Art object symbolizing family spirit.

Selected Bibliography

SPECIAL QUOTATIONS AND INTERNET TOPICS

(a) All bible quotations are from King James Version.

(b) http://www.oi.uchicago.edu/OI/PROJ/NUB/NUBX92?NUBX92-fig2.html

(c) Lost Nubia: A Centennial Exhibit of Photographs From the 1905–1907 Egyptian Expeditions of the University of Chicago, front cover and catalog #45 (pages 90 and 91).

(d) Saba: http://www.Kessler-web.co.uk/History/Kinglists... 1999- Kessler associates.

(e) Aksum: http://en.wikipedia.org/wiki/kingdom_of_Aksum. From Wikipedia, the free encyclopedia.

(f) Jos Plateau: http://en.wikipedia.org/wiki/jos_Plateau. 1999-

(g) African Literature: http://en.wikipedia.org/wiki/AfricanLiterature ; http://www .africanlit.com/.

(h) African Art and Architecture: http://encarta.msn.com/encyclopedia_761574805 /African_Art_and_Architecture.html. 2003.

(i) Oil Palm Tree: http://en.wikipedia.org/wiki/Palm_oil; http://en.wikipedia.org /wiki/oil_palm.

BOOKS CONSULTED

Achebe, C. *Girls at War and other Stories*, (New York, Anchor Books, 1987).

———. *Things Fall Apart*. (New York, Astor-Honor, 1959)

Afigbo, A. E. *Igbo History and Society: Essays*. (Trenton NJ. African World Press, 2005).

———. *Igbo Genesis*. (Uturu, Abia State University Press for Center for Igbo Studies, 2001).

——. *The age of innocence: The Igbo and Their Neighbors in pre-colonial times*. (Paper presented at Ahiajoku Lecture Series; 1981), Pages 6–27.

Alaezi, O. Ibos: *Hebrew exiles from Israel; Amazing Revelations*; (Aba Nigeria, Onzy Publications, 1999).

Bianchi, Robert S. *Daily life of Nubians*: (The Greenwood Press daily life through history series, 2004) pp 102–103.

Bowers, Paul. *Nubian Christianity: The Neglected Heritage*; (African Journal of Evangelical Theology iv. 1, 1985) 3–23.

Derek, A. W. and Julie R. Anderson. *Sudan's Ancient Treasures*; (British Museum Press, 2004).

Diop, C. A. *The African Origin of Civilization; Myth or Reality ;(* London, Lawrence Hill Books, 1974).

Emecheta B. *Destination Biafra*. African Writers Series. (London, Heinemann 1982).

Fage, J.D. and R. A. Oliver Eds. Papers in African prehistory. (London, Cambridge University Press, 1970)

Forsyth, F. *The making of an African Legend: The Biafra Story*. London, Penguin Books, 1969)

Ike, A. 1951. *The Origin of Igbos*. (Aba Nigeria, Silent Prayer Home Press 1951).

Ikeanyibe, U. C. *Hebrew and Biblical Sources of Igbo History*. Benin City Nigeria, Seed Sowers Publications, 1999).

Isichei, Elizabeth. *A History of the Igbo People*. (New York, London St. Martin's Press, Inc., 1976)

——. *Igbo World: an anthology of oral histories and historical description*. (Philadelphia, Institute for the study of human resources, 1978).

Madu, R. O. *African Symbols, Proverbs and Myths: the Hermeneutics of destiny*. (New York, P. Lang Publications, 1992).

Morkot, Robert G. *The Black Pharaohs: Egypt's Nubian Rulers*. (W.M. Flinders Petrie, A history of Egypt, Part three 1896, 2000) pp 278–279.

Njoku, J. E. *A dictionary of Igbo names, culture and proverbs*. (Washington, University Press of America, 1978).

Nwadinigwe, P. J. O. *The Origin of Igbo: Perspective on the history, Socio-cultural and the religious life of Igbos. (*Amawbia, Anambra State Lumos Nigerian Ltd., 1999).

Ogbalu, F. C. *Ilu Igbo: The book of Igbo proverbs*. (Onitsha Nigeria, University Pub. Co., 1965).

Ottenberg, S. and Toyin Falola. 2006. *Igbo Religion, Social Life and other essays*; Trenton New Jersey, African World Press, 2006.

Seligma, O.C. *Races of Africa*. London, Oxford University Press, 1978.

http://en.wikipedia.org/wiki/kingdom_of_Aksum

Stuart Munro-Hay, "Aksum: An African Civilization of Late Antiquity. Edinburgh: University Press 1991, pp.57.

Index

119

About the Author

Chukwuma Obiagwu is currently, the Director of NovaNET (Digital Learning Systems) at Little Rock School District in Arkansas. Professionally, he is a scientist and an educator who taught applied sciences at the University of Agriculture at Makurdi Nigeria and University of Arkansas at Pine Bluff Arkansas. He also taught pure sciences at various public schools in Arkansas. As a Scientist, Dr. Obiagwu published several articles in the area of "Soil Fertility Managements" in many International Journals. He is also the current General Secretary of "Ndigbo in Arkansas", a nonprofit public corporation. In that capacity, he has travel the length and breath of the United States for purposes of promoting Igbo Culture in Diaspora. He grew up in Igbo land and served in Biafran Military at age 14. At the end of civil war, he came to the United States to attend higher education. He has been back to Nigeria as a Senior Lecturer at the University of Agriculture where he experienced first hand, the mistreatment of Igbos in Nigerian State as a result of the loss of Biafra. He came back to Arkansas where he eventually settled to welcome his kinsmen who might want Arkansas as their home also. He is making an effort to ensure that while in personal exile, his descendants will never forget the culture of Igbo people.

/